Bonnie,

The secret to change is
to focus all of your the
energy not on fighting the
old, but on building the new.

Wishing you all the best,

Bob Johnson
8-11-14

Facing the
SUNSHINE
and Avoiding the
SHADOWS

*Strategies to Stay Sane
and Positive amid Change*

Becky Johnen

[signature] 8-11-14

InspiringVoices®
A Service of **Guideposts**

Inspiring Voices books may be ordered through booksellers or by contacting:

Inspiring Voices
1663 Liberty Drive
Bloomington, IN 47403
www.inspiringvoices.com
1-(866) 697-5313

ISBN: 978-1-4624-0746-0 (sc)
ISBN: 978-1-4624-0747-7 (e)

Library of Congress Control Number: 2013916847

Printed in the United States of America.

Inspiring Voices rev. date: 9/24/2013

To my mom and dad for laying the groundwork.
To my husband, Bob, for his support, love, and understanding.
To St. Elias Byzantine Catholic Church's Bethany Ministry
participants for their inspiration and motivation.

Table of Contents

Preface

THIS BOOK CAME ABOUT because of a conference presentation. During the 1980s and early '90s, I was working at Chemeketa Community College in Salem, Oregon, as the associate dean for developmental education. In 1993, I relocated to my home state of Pennsylvania, where I took a position as dean for the Lebanon campus of Harrisburg Area Community College. During this same time, I was very active in the College Reading and Learning Association (CRLA), frequently presenting at its conferences.

Also during this time, I watched my staff and colleagues become frustrated, angry, depressed, fearful, and stressed over changes happening in postsecondary education. How best to help those with whom I worked most closely became a passion of mine. In fact, for the CRLA's 1997 annual conference (whose theme was "Pearls of Wisdom"), I submitted a proposal to speak on dealing with change. But what focus should that presentation take?

The inspiration for the focus of the presentation came while sitting on an airplane and waiting for it to depart. The flight attendant was going through her preflight instructions and said, "The cabin is pressurized for your comfort, but in the event of an emergency, oxygen masks will automatically appear. If you are traveling with young children, *put your own oxygen mask on first and then put the mask on your children."*

Aha, I thought. *That is it.*

That is it. Those instructions got me to thinking about taking care of ourselves, especially in our daily lives since we tend to go around putting "oxygen masks" on everyone else. Sometimes, we forget to put our own oxygen mask on first. Oxygen rejuvenates; it gives us stamina. If we don't start taking care of ourselves first, we can become depleted, drained, and burned out. We need stamina to deal with everyday challenges, such as those that I saw my staff and colleagues facing. These challenges included being asked to do more and more with less and less, having many needs but not enough resources to meet those needs, and being asked to do the impossible.

Life presents many challenges, and we admirably deal with these, but at what cost to our personal well-being? As challenges mount, we often feel stressed and depleted of energy. It's all the little things, all of the things that stack one by one on top of us. It's like the saying, "You can get nibbled to death by ducks. No one takes a big bite, but all those nibbles eventually get to you." So that this doesn't happen, we need to be conscious of what "oxygenates" us, what keeps us going. And we need to make a conscious effort to pay attention to the warning signs of oxygen depletion and get that mask on in time, so we don't collapse.

To effectively deal with change, we must first take care of ourselves before we can even think about negotiating the change or helping others work in the new/changed environment. How do we take care of ourselves? A quote from Helen Keller—"Keep your face to the sunshine and you will never see the shadow"—came to mind, and my presentation on change had its focus (Keller 2013). I titled the presentation "Facing the Sunshine and Avoiding the Shadows: Strategies to Stay Sane and Positive amid Change."

The presentation highlighted sixteen strategies for dealing with change, sixteen "oxygen sources" to face the sunshine and avoid the shadows. To help participants remember the strategies, PRESERVING SANITY served as an acronym, with each letter representing a strategy. (There is no significance to the order of the strategies.) This book puts to print the ideas shared in that 1997 conference presentation as well as those that have come about after sixteen years of speaking on the topic.

To those who read this book, it is my heartfelt wish that there are some pearls of wisdom that help when undergoing change and transition or just help with daily life issues.

Acknowledgments

I AM INDEBTED TO Jimmy Pickett, a friend who took time from his private practice as a psychologist to critique sections of the book. Through his insight, wisdom, and professional expertise, he has helped make this book a much stronger and more useful resource. You are truly a touchstone in my life.

Dr. Bill Segura, who served as president of Chemeketa Community College from the early 1980s until the early 1990s, was an outstanding mentor. I am grateful to him for all the lessons on leadership and organizational change and for bringing Dr. William Bridges to our campus. The lessons Bridges taught us have remained with me all these years and have had a profound and positive influence on my leadership style as well as my view of change/transition.

Over the past thirty years, the College Reading and Learning Association (CRLA) has provided many learning opportunities for me, including providing a forum for the sharing of ideas. I am so appreciative of all my CRLA colleagues. I especially want to thank Dr. Karen Agee for her unique way of looking at things and for her support and inspiration. I also want to note my appreciation of Dr. Valerie Smith-Stephens for her notes of encouragement and motivation.

Change: What Is It, and Why Is It So Difficult?

"Change is the essence of life. Be willing to surrender
what you are for what you could become."
—Unknown

To change, in its simplest form, is to make something different
from what it is. No matter how small or dramatic the change, it is
accompanied by fear, doubt, and uncertainty. Sure, we see the need
for something in our lives or profession to change; however, many
don't want to move out of our comfort zones. The comfort zone is
like a child's security blanket: we feel safe and secure when wrapped
in the zone.

Many people become unsettled by or fear change because of
the unknown. We don't know what is coming. We feel safe with
predictability, sureness, and the routine. Change is like opening a
door and not having any idea of what is on the other side; we step into
the unknown. We lose that comfortable routine, that comfort zone,
and that is scary and frightening.

William Bridges, author of *Managing Transitions: Making the Most
of Change* (1991), talks about change being situational; it is something

that happens to us. Examples of situational changes with which we commonly deal include relocating to a new home, moving from one school to another, starting a new job, retiring, getting married/divorced/widowed, and having a child.

In each of those examples, there is an element of unknown. No matter how excited we may be about the new opportunity each change may bring about, we have moments of doubt, fear, and unease, all caused by the move out of our comfort zone and not knowing what may happen. Bridges refers to the emotional or psychological component of this change process as "transitions." According to Bridges, transitions are what we experience as we internalize and come to terms with the details of the new situation that comes with the change. And Bridges feels that it is the transition and not the change that unsettles people.

Both the change itself (the physical aspect) and the transitions (the psychological aspect) combine to make us feel the frustration, anger, depression, fear, and stress that accompany dealing with whatever is becoming different in our lives. A good example is the first time I felt fear. I grew up in West Mifflin, Pennsylvania, home to Kennywood Park, a local amusement park. As a child, I was fascinated by the roller coasters and migrated from the benign ones in Kiddie Land to the faster, steeper ones in the park. On all but one, the ups, downs, and curves in the track were visible and I could mentally prepare for what was coming. That was not the case with the Pippin. This coaster had a tunnel, and for first-time riders, what came after the tunnel was unknown. I went from loving the thrill of the coasters to being scared to death of this one. The addition of the tunnel (the physical change to the coaster) and not knowing what to expect at the end of it (the psychological aspect) caused me to move out of the personal comfort zone I had created with the other more predictable coasters; I feared getting on this one.

The fear of change is the greatest roadblock to change. It is why so many people put up so much resistance to the thought of change. Much of the resistance stems from how the change is perceived: good/bad; minor/major/seismic; small effect/huge effect; fair/unfair; positive/negative. Letting go of the fear is the easy answer to dealing with change. However, letting go is easier said than done. Since change is a constant in our lives, we need to learn to accept it and to embrace it. Developing skills to cope with and to respond to the changes/transitions in our lives is critical if we want to lead happy, productive lives.

Reader Reflection

1. What is change?
2. What is transition?
3. Why does change feel so difficult at times?
4. What does change mean to me?
5. What changes are happening in my life?
6. How are these changes making me feel?
7. Am I prepared to respond to or cope with these changes? If not, what do I need to do? If so, in what ways am I prepared?
8. Do I fear these changes? If so, why? What should I do to overcome my fears?

PRESERVING SANITY:
Persistence

"In the confrontation between the stream and the rock, the stream always wins. Not through strength, but through persistence."
—Unknown

PERSISTENCE IS DOGGED DETERMINATION, tenacity, and perseverance. It is the ability to keep on going no matter what one may be facing or how one feels about the situation. Why is persistence important when dealing with change? When we get overwhelmed by what is happening or paralyzed by being forced out of our comfort zones, it is easy for us to just give in or give up. Neither of those is an option when change is upon us. Neither of those helps us in dealing with what faces us. It is our ability to keep moving forward, to persist even in the face of adversity, that will help us continually move forward.

The power of persistence was never more evident to me than when I first saw Arch Rock in Oceanside on the Oregon Coast. Arch Rock is named for its shape. I watched as the waves relentlessly pounded at the rock and wondered how something as soft and pliable as water could make a hole in something as hard and unyielding as rock. It dawned on me that it wasn't the water itself creating the hole but the persistence of the waves upon the rock. The persistent wash of water upon the once solid rock carved it into a sight to behold. Another aha moment: the force of the waves is in their persistence. If the persistent action of something like water can alter a solid material, just think of what our collective and persistent efforts can achieve!

When we are not excited by a change or are fearful of what the change might bring, it is easy to lose sight of where we are going or to lose motivation for what we are doing. Persistence helps us maintain action and helps us produce results. Steve Pavlina, author of *Personal Development for Smart People*, in his blog on self-discipline and persistence, says, "The value of persistence comes not from stubbornly clinging to the past. It comes from a vision of the future that's so compelling you would give almost anything to make it real" (2006).

While there may be comfort for us in the past or the old, we can't get rooted in it. We need to be able to continually move forward despite the difficulties created by the change. Persistence helps us become resolute in doing this; it gives us the resolve to go on; it provides the drive.

What can we do to develop this skill, this strategy?

1. Study successful people. Think of people who persisted despite the odds (e.g., Gandhi, Martin Luther King Jr., Beethoven, and Abraham Lincoln). Make a list of what they did to persist in the wake of what they were facing.
2. Have a wish, dream, or goal. What is it we want to see happen or hope to accomplish? Write the wish or dream down, and if you have more than one, prioritize them. Remember that wishes with planning become goals. Goals provide us with a purpose. And goals with persistence become achievements.
3. Have a plan for how the wishes/dreams/goals will be reached. Outline the steps that will be needed to reach each wish/dream/goal.

4. Remain upbeat and positive. Maintaining a positive outlook is crucial in developing persistence. The time, setbacks, and the energy drain can all take a toll and weaken one's resolve.

5. Stay focused and motivated. Being persistent is not easy, and it is not quick. One must be determined, focused, and motivated to keep on task, no matter what else is going on. Total commitment to the purpose of the task is needed.

6. Learn to jump hurdles. Life would be great if it were all smooth sailing. When developing persistence, expect some rough waters along the way, some speed bumps, and some roadblocks. Have strategies in place to handle the unexpected, such as hearing no a lot and meeting resistance.

7. Develop a support network. Make sure there is a strong connection with at least one person who can provide encouragement and motivation. Those in this network should be considered accountability managers.

Reader Reflection

1. What is persistence?
2. Why is this strategy an important one when dealing with change/transition?
3. When would it be good to use this strategy?
4. Which of the development suggestions would be most effective for me? Why?
5. Think about family, friends, and colleagues. Are there any who exemplify persistence? Create a list of how they are persistent. Are there characteristics on the list I would find helpful in my situation?
6. Am I facing a change where persistence is needed?
7. Am I prepared to be persistent? If so, in what way(s)? If not, what do I need to do?

8. If I am already a persistent person, are there things I can do to strengthen the skill?
9. Is this a skill I need to develop? If so, select at least one of the suggestions from the above list to focus on.
10. How do I see myself using this strategy when dealing with change/transition?
11. Even if not undergoing a change or transition, how can I apply this strategy to my daily life to make it more meaningful, pleasant, and positive?

pReserving Sanity:
Relationships

"It takes a lot of understanding, time, and trust to gain a close friendship with someone. As I approach a time of my life of complete uncertainty, my friends are my most precious asset."
—Unknown

THE STRATEGY OF RELATIONSHIPS focuses on friendship and having people with whom we can interact in our lives. Friendship is often defined as the relationship between people characterized by assistance, approval, and support. It is a connection between people where key components include trust, concern, care, and understanding.

Why are relationships important when dealing with change? Oftentimes, change brings some chaos, turmoil, and disruption to our lives. What better time to have a "touchstone" in our lives—someone to share what we're going through, someone with whom to vent, and someone to just listen to how we feel. If the change is viewed in a positive way, friends can help us celebrate the good; if viewed in a negative way, friends can help us through the tough moments.

Tough moments can lead to stress, which can be a frequent visitor during times of change. Friends provide a measure of stability that is most helpful when dealing with the stress associated with the change or the accompanying transitions. They listen, they encourage, they provide suggestions and advice, and they are just there to provide whatever support may be needed.

A good example of this comes from a time in my personal life when I was going through the toughest of changes: the death of my mother. My mother had been battling breast cancer, and when we got word that she had only two months to live, I took a leave of absence from my job so I could become her full-time caregiver. Not only was I dealing with all the emotions that one goes through in preparing for the death of a loved one, but also I was doing so at a distance from friends and family. My two closest friends—both quite far away, with one living near Oklahoma City, Oklahoma, and one near Harrisburg, Pennsylvania— kept in close and constant touch by phone during these two months. And in the last week of my mother's life, my Oklahoma friend called every single day to check on me and to provide emotional support.

Our friendships, and all of our relationships, provide us with a measure of collaboration, connection, and coalition when dealing with change. This is like people in a maze trying to find their way out. If my friend and I are in the maze together and working on our own to find the way out, we would struggle because we can't see what is ahead or around a corner. However, if one gets on the shoulders of the other, perhaps we could see over the barriers of the maze and give directions like, "Turn right and then right again and we'll be out." This type of collaboration or coalition is value added; it is synergistic in the sense that the two of us created a result that would be different from or greater than what each of us could have done individually. What a positive and productive way of dealing with change and transition.

Already have close friends? What can be done to maintain those relationships or to strengthen them, hence strengthening this strategy? No close circle of friends? What can be done to develop this skill, this strategy of relationship?

1. Stay in contact with best/good friends. I feel it is best to do so personally through visits, phone calls, and handwritten letters. If time or distance prevents doing these, then use social media venues, such as Facebook or Twitter, and/or send e-mails or texts to keep the connection active.

2. Develop a circle of friends; meet people. This is done primarily in two ways: situational, such as at school, church, and work, or through interests done in one's spare time, such as hobbies (book clubs, cooking classes, video gaming, wellness activities, etc.).

3. Consider what is needed from the relationship. There are different types of relationships/friendships, and each can provide different levels of support during times of change. I have known my two closest friends since elementary school. We've been close for more than fifty years, and these friends do it all and do it on a deep and emotional level. They listen, they encourage, they provide advice and suggestions, and they provide support. I make it a point to stay in close contact with these two whether in person, on the phone, or online. On the other hand, I have work friends, church friends, lacrosse friends, Jazzercise friends, and gym friends—people I may only see in those contexts. These are friends who may do the same things my closest friends do, but not on such a deep or emotional level. They may only deal with specific issues, and oftentimes, these issues relate to the context in which I know them.

4. Make friends by being a friend. Be a friend by reflecting on the qualities that make a good friend and actively practicing them. In other words, apply the Golden Rule: "Do unto others as you would have them do unto you." Show respect

for others; show gratitude for others. Listen, share, care, celebrate, cry, laugh, and show "tough love" when needed.

Reader Reflection

1. On what does the strategy of relationships focus?
2. Why is this strategy an important one when dealing with change/transition?
3. When would it be good to use this strategy?
4. Which of the development suggestions would be most effective for me? Why?
5. Think about current friends. Why are they included in my circle of friends?
6. Do I communicate regularly with my friends?
7. Am I facing a change where a strong relationship/friend is needed?
8. Which of my friends are touchstones? Why do I feel that way?
9. Is this a skill I need to develop? If yes, select at least one of the suggestions from the above list to focus on.
10. If I am a friend, are there things I can do to strengthen the relationship? Things I can do to be a better friend?
11. How do I see myself using this strategy when dealing with change/transition?
12. Even if not undergoing a change or transition, how can I apply this strategy to my daily life to make it more meaningful, pleasant, and positive?

PR**E**SERVING SANITY:
Enthusiasm

"Enthusiasm releases the drive to carry you over
obstacles and adds significance to all you do."
—Norman Vincent Peale

THE STRATEGY OF ENTHUSIASM focuses on the need to remain positive and upbeat at all times. Again, think about what happens when we encounter change. Something is different; things may be chaotic; we are being moved away from our comfort zone. Whenever there is change, issues will arise, and it is easy to give up and give in to the issue. If we can maintain excitement and enthusiasm, we are able to effectively deal with whatever issue the change may be presenting.

When dealing with change, enthusiasm can make the difference between success and failure. If we mope and fight the change, we may be doomed. If we cope and look for ways to coexist with the change, we will thrive. Coping and coexisting with change may mean we need to be creative to do so, and enthusiasm can generate creativity that can lead to innovation, which can lead to coming up with ways of effectively and positively dealing with change.

Enthusiasm is contagious and can spread from person to person quickly and easily. It is difficult to be around someone who is positive and upbeat and has a zest for life without some of that same feeling catching hold of us. This is always a good thing when one is dealing with something that is stressful, chaotic, or unpleasant.

My role models for this strategy are young children at play. Watch them and their unbridled enthusiasm for all that they do. Young children are naturally enthusiastic and happy about everything. When serving as a head of a private school, I often observed classes. I noticed that preschool and primary-level children were always enthusiastically willing to answer questions. The question didn't matter. All hands would shoot into the air and would be waving while their eyes (and sometimes their voices) would implore, "Pick me! Pick me!"

I noticed a dramatic difference with the older elementary children, beginning around age ten. If I asked any question, a few hands shot up. Many children would look around to see what others were doing. Some hands tentatively were raised. The body language changed significantly. Many heads and eyes were lowered. Rarely would there be eager chants of "Pick me!"

The difference here is that the younger children were so enthusiastic about learning (learning is still "play" to them) and so willing to share they didn't care what anyone else thought, nor did they care if they were right or wrong. Around age ten, being right or wrong becomes a huge issue. Saving face in front of peers is huge, hence the hesitation to respond. The enthusiasm for sharing is not the same.

It is critical that we never lose our ability to remain enthusiastic about life and what it may present to us. We need to maintain this childlike level of exuberance and do so especially when dealing with change. The ability to remain positive and upbeat when the issues associated with change and transition move us out of our comfort zone is vital to us coming through the change or transition healthy, content, and in one piece.

What can we do to develop this skill, this strategy?

1. Be positive, and practice positive thinking. Look for the good and positive in everything. I have a philosophy that there is no such thing as a bad day. There may be bad moments in a day, but there can't be twenty-four hours of bad. When faced with something one might consider bad, turn it around and look for the good or positive in it. Enthusiasm thrives in a positive environment. Surround yourself with enthusiastic people.

2. Avoid "energy vampires." Energy vampires are people who maintain a negative attitude about most everything in life, and they can suck the enthusiasm right out of other people. They are the doom and gloom people who never seem to be able to find the good or positive in anything. A positive outlook cannot be developed or maintained in the wake of negative thoughts. Negativity breeds negativity and can permeate all aspects of one's being. Steer clear of the energy vampires while looking at the bright side of things. Being positive breeds being positive and will feed enthusiasm.

3. Love who you are and what you do; maintain a passion for life. When talking to students thinking about their career choice, I would always advise them to select something that they are passionate about. I asked them to think about the number of Monday mornings or Friday afternoons they would be working. They are way too many not to absolutely love the work one does. The passion for and love of life and what we do in it only build enthusiasm.

4. Adopt a "gratitude attitude." Robert A. Emmons (2013) writes about developing a "gratitude attitude." This is a strategy where we acknowledge what we are grateful or thankful for. Doing this will often help with becoming more excited about or enthusiastic about who we are, what we are doing, and what we are facing. When we are grateful for things, stuff that

overwhelms us (a lot of the stuff that may accompany change) isn't able to take front and center stage. Being grateful helps put us in a positive emotional mind-set and helps generate enthusiasm. Gratitude can energize us at the start of a day as well as relax us at the close of a day. Reflecting on the good things in our lives helps us maintain perspective and helps us deal with whatever rough patches change and transition may throw our way.

5. *Don't Sweat the Small Stuff* (Carlson, 1997). Nothing dampens enthusiasm quicker than worry, especially worrying about things over which we have no control. Let go of trying to "change the change" and instead focus energy on dealing with the change: find solutions to the issues. You will know if you are moving in the right direction because you will be enthusiastic about where you are heading.

Reader Reflection

1. On what does the strategy of enthusiasm focus?
2. Why are young children good role models for this strategy?
3. What is a "gratitude attitude"?
4. What is an "energy vampire"? Are there any in my life? If yes, am I effectively dealing with them? What can I do to become more effective in dealing with them?
5. Why is this strategy an important one when dealing with change and transition?
6. When would it be good to use this strategy?
7. Which of the development suggestions would be most effective for me? Why?
8. Am I facing a change where enthusiasm is needed?
9. Am I prepared to be enthusiastic in the wake of change? If yes, in what way(s)? If no, what do I need to do?

10. If I am already a pretty enthusiastic person, are there things I can do to strengthen the skill?

11. Is this a skill I need to develop? If yes, select at least one of the suggestions from the above list to focus on.

12. How do I see myself using this strategy when dealing with change/transition?

13. Even if not undergoing a change or transition, how can I apply this strategy to my daily life to make it more meaningful, pleasant, and positive?

PRESERVING SANITY:
Sense of Humor

"Nobody says you must laugh, but a sense of humor can
help you overlook the unattractive, tolerate the unpleasant,
cope with the unexpected, and smile through the day."
—Ann Landers

THE STRATEGY OF SENSE of humor highlights the need to laugh
a lot, to laugh often, and to lighten the day with levity. A sense of
humor also means that we are able to see the humor in the craziness
of life. This is a strategy that truly helps us preserve our sanity when
things get chaotic or we get overwhelmed with the stress that might
come with change and transition. Using our sense of humor is a
very effective coping mechanism and an easy stress-management
technique.

There is no doubt that there are many challenges when dealing
with change and transition. When our comfort zone shifts, it is easy
to feel as if the world has fallen out from under us. This strategy can
help us feel as if we are on firm ground again and help shift us back
into or closer to our comfort zone. Laugher is often the result when

we exercise our sense of humor. Laughing can help us deal with the most difficult of situations.

When undergoing change and transition, we sometimes feel as if we have no control; the forces of change have taken away our "power." Stress and tension are a result of this. A sense of humor has a way of putting us back in the driver's seat, helping us regain some control, dispel the tension, and relieve the stress. Because change and transition are often accompanied by emotional and mental stress, humor and its accompanying laughter help keep our emotional, mental, and even physical health in balance. Humor can help us develop peace of mind, hopefulness, joy, cheerfulness, resilience, an uplifted spirit, and a good sense of life.

I have already mentioned dealing with the life-changing situation for me: learning that my mom had two weeks to live and being her caregiver during this time. Talk about tension, stress, and lack of control. However, it was my mom and her sense of humor that provided a much-needed measure of comfort for me. She wanted to die at home, and with the help of hospice, we were able to honor that wish. We had a hospital bed placed in the living room for her, and the recliner became my bed.

One morning near the end, my mom woke up, looked over at me, and asked what I was doing there. I explained that I was there to help her through this part of her life's journey. She stated, "You mean I'm not dead yet?" I told her no, that that time hadn't yet come. She turned her eyes up toward heaven and shouted, "Have you forgotten about me?" We both laughed and hugged and laughed, but the tension of the overall situation was lightened considerably by her outlook on things.

How else can a sense of humor help us when dealing with change and transition? A good sense of humor can help us keep things in perspective. If we remember that we aren't the only ones undergoing changes and transitions, having a sense of humor about life's difficulties can help us become closer to those dealing with the same or a similar situation. In a way, this helps bring a measure of normalcy to what one is experiencing. Whatever we may be dealing with may not seem so overwhelming or frightening.

How many of you have failed to back up work on the computer? I am so guilty of this. I remember working on my doctoral dissertation in the wee hours of the morning, typing away and not backing up at all. (And I was doing a "download" from what was in my head and on note cards, not just typing from something I had handwritten.) All of a sudden, there was a very short power glitch. When I rebooted the computer, nothing I had worked on for quite some time was there. I just sat there looking at the screen, wondering whether I should laugh, cry, or give up.

I quickly phoned a close friend in Oregon (the time difference worked for me; it was only 11 p.m. there) and shared my frustration over what had just happened. She, in her no nonsense way, told me that what just happened was God's way of letting me what I had just typed was "crap" and that I was to get a fresh start. We both started laughing. Through the laughter, she talked about how many times she had done this only to regroup and come out better and stronger afterward.

Her sense of humor did, indeed, help put things in perspective for me. I picked up the pieces and moved forward with my work, and it was far better than what I had done prior to the power glitch.

Don't have a sense of humor or would like to strengthen it? What can be done to develop the sense of humor strategy?

1. Reframe the situation. Take whatever is changing or the part of the change that is creating stress and find a humorous way of looking at that situation. Television sitcoms have a wonderful way of reframing life situations. Watch one to see what they do and then apply the same or similar techniques to find the humor in the personal situation.

2. Rise above the situation. Remain objective and avoid becoming a victim to the change. When my mom got

diagnosed with breast cancer and had her first mastectomy, my husband and I visited her in the hospital. What in the world do you say to someone who has just undergone this life-changing procedure? My mom beat all of us to the punch, announcing, "Now my garden rows will have a reason to be crooked!" Again, it was her sense of humor that helped all of us. But most of all, it helped her in not becoming a victim to the circumstance.

3. Reflect on personal moments that were embarrassing and find the humor in them. During my wedding ceremony, when I walked to place flowers at the statue of the Blessed Mother, my matron of honor was to slightly lift the train of my dress just enough that I wouldn't trip over it. Well, she gave new meaning to "slightly lift" when my undergarments were exposed for all to see. Embarrassing? To the extreme. How was I going to deal with this at the reception? I just told everyone it was our way of showing my mom that I had listened to her about the need to always wear clean underwear! That comment saved face for everyone involved. (And yes, that person is still one of my two best friends in the world.)

4. Read books, watch shows, or visit websites that take normal events many would find annoying, frustrating, upsetting, or overwhelming and show how silly the situation or reaction to the situation is. Television sitcoms are notorious for doing this on a regular basis. Late-night talk shows hosts are masters of this with their monologues. Comedians make a living doing this. Cartoons of the 1950s and 1960s are classics at this.

5. Develop a humor bulletin board. Make space on the refrigerator, a wall, the side of a file cabinet, or wherever there is space in the house or the office. Post comics, signs, funny sayings, bumper stickers, or anything else that points out the

humor in something. When change or transition is getting to be too much, take a moment to check out the humor board. If nothing else, it should bring about a smile.

Reader Reflection

1. On what does the strategy of sense of humor focus?
2. In what ways can a sense of humor help me cope with the stress that might accompany change?
3. How can a sense of humor help me keep things in perspective?
4. Why is this strategy an important one when dealing with change/transition?
5. When would it be good to use this strategy?
6. Which of the development suggestions would be most effective for me? Why?
7. Am I facing a change where a sense of humor is needed?
8. Am I prepared to have a sense of humor in the wake of change? If yes, in what way(s)? If no, what do I need to do?
9. If I already have a pretty decent sense of humor, are there things I can do to strengthen the skill?
10. Is this a skill I need to develop? If yes, select at least one of the suggestions from the above list to focus on.
11. How do I see myself using this strategy when dealing with change/transition?
12. Even if not undergoing a change or transition, how can I apply this strategy to my daily life to make it more meaningful, pleasant, and positive?

PRESERVING SANITY:
Ending Something

"All transitions begin with endings."
—William Bridges

THE FIRST CHAPTER OF this book introduced change and why it is so difficult. That same chapter introduced the work of William Bridges (1991, 2004). According to Bridges, change is situational. Something starts or something stops. Change that is unfinished or gradual is often referred to as "transition," but in his work, Bridges refers to this type of transition as a "changeover" process that is made up of a series of different steps that take place at different times and that are in themselves little changes.

Bridges refers to the emotional or psychological component of this change process as "transitions." According to Bridges, transitions are what we go through as we internalize and come to terms with the details of the new situation that comes with the change. In his work, there are three predictable stages in the transition process. Ending something is the first of these three stages, and it is the next strategy we will explore in managing and surviving change.

Why is ending something important when dealing with change? To get what one wants, one must give up what is. All change, all transitions, begin with endings and with losses. In relocating to a new community, living in one's house and neighborhood ends. In divorce, a relationship ends. When computers entered the scene, use of typewriters went by the wayside. In a job promotion, the familiar job ends. I started my professional career as a classroom teacher. After several years, I wanted to move into administration, but I also didn't want to not be a classroom teacher. However, to reach my goal of an administrator, I had to end being a classroom teacher (at least a full-time teacher). I had to give up what was to get what I wanted.

Each of these examples came with a loss: loss of familiar routines, loss of a familiar way of doing something, loss of a relationship, loss of a comfort zone, perhaps even loss of control, space, power, social/role identity, or influence. It is important to accept this sense of loss and the emotions felt because of the loss: anger, resentment, sadness, and resistance. In order to be able to fully let go and embrace what the change brings, the acceptance of the loss, of the end of the current, is vital.

What can be done to help people let go, to develop the strategy of ending something?

1. Acknowledge the loss. Talk about the loss with others. Talk about what the loss means. Communicate the feelings the loss is generating.
2. Grieve for what has been lost or what has been let go. While everyone grieves differently and more like a roller coaster than in discreet stages, the stages in the Kübler-Ross model (2005) are a helpful guide. Those stages are denial, anger bargaining, depression, and acceptance.
3. Use rituals to help overcome the loss. A commonly used ritual is a party: birthday, retirement, farewell, New Year's Eve, wedding showers, bachelor parties, funeral wakes, etc.

4. Ask questions: Who? What? When? How? Why? Who will be affected by this? What is going to happen? When is it going to happen? How will all this happen? Why is it going to happen?

Reader Reflection

1. With respect to change, what does ending something mean?
2. In what ways does ending something help when undergoing change?
3. What are the similarities between ending something and the grieving process?
4. Why is this strategy an important one when dealing with change/transition?
5. When would it be good to use this strategy?
6. Which of the development suggestions would be most effective for me? Why?
7. Am I facing a change where something needs to be ended?
8. Am I prepared to end something in the wake of change? If yes, in what way(s)? If no, what do I need to do?
9. Is this a skill I need to develop? If yes, select at least one of the suggestions from the above list to focus on.
10. How do I see myself using this strategy when dealing with change/transition?
11. Even if not undergoing a change or transition, how can I apply this strategy to my daily life to make it more meaningful, pleasant, and positive?

PRESE**R**VING SANITY:
Roaming the Wilderness

"Creativity can be described as letting go of certainties."
—Gail Sheehy

THE STRATEGY OF ROAMING the wilderness is what William Bridges (1991, 2004) calls the "neutral zone" and is the second step in his transition process. The neutral zone is a place where the old and the new overlap. I liken this neutral zone to what the early pioneers felt when they ventured beyond their "comfort zone." For them, there was a lot of confusion with new sights, sounds, and experiences. The rules they followed in their former place no longer applied, yet new rules for this new territory, this "wilderness," had not yet been established. The farther they got on their journey, they could no longer see where they came from and they couldn't see exactly where they were going. At times, there was probably a sense of feeling lost, and at other times, these pioneers had to gain a new sense of direction. There had to be much fear of the unknown in the new, changed environment.

Why, if this neutral zone is so "wild" and further engenders confusion and fear, is it important when dealing with change? It is because out of the confusion and fear, new ideas, new discoveries, reorientations, and creativity take center stage and help propel those undergoing the change toward something they might be able to accept, something that might make their life better.

In the last chapter, I shared that in my professional career, I had to end being a classroom teacher to reach my goal of becoming an administrator. I had already moved from being a middle school and high school classroom teacher to teaching at the community college level. In that change, I did let go of the familiar with the age and level of students, but that change was not as dramatic as moving into the realm of administration. While I had an idea of what college administrators did, I really didn't know what my administrative role would look or feel like.

After accepting my first college administrative position, I did roam the wilderness. I was still in the educational arena, but it was so different. No bell schedule. No students at their seats. No lesson planning. No trying to decide the best active learning strategy for the class. Meetings, budgets, motivating staff, dealing with human resource issues—yikes! Talk about being frightened, confused, and scared.

I tried a lot of things. Some of them were quite successful; others, not so much. Many times, I thought I was definitely on the right track to a breakthrough of sorts, only to have everything fall flat. Yet through it all, I learned how to translate the success I had in the classroom into how to become an effective administrator. Roaming the wilderness, navigating the neutral zone, definitely helped me find myself in the administrative role and become a better and more effective person in that role.

How can one "roam the wilderness" safely? How does one develop this skill?

1. Experiment with the ideas that come to the surface. Use trial and error in deciding what to do, what direction in which to go, and whom to see.

2. Reward and reinforce. After trying something, whether it is a success or a failure, give the thumbs-up or words of encouragement. Treating oneself or others to something is a nice acknowledgment of the efforts. Giving out something that is symbolic of whatever was tried provides a reward as well as a visual reminder of the effort.
3. Be patient. Give others and yourself time to work through the thoughts, ideas, and suggestions. Periodically, step back and evaluate all that has been going on while roaming the wilderness.
4. Talk, talk, and talk some more. Talk about feelings, fears, frustrations, anxieties, and ideas.
5. Be observant. Watch for "footprints in the snow" or those signs of how things are evolving. Capitalize on the moments of creativity.
6. Set short-term goals. Where do things need to be in a day? A week? At the end of the month? What should things look like in a day, week, or month?

Reader Reflection

1. What does it mean to roam the wilderness or be in a neutral zone?
2. Why is this strategy an important one when dealing with change/transition?
3. When would it be good to use this strategy?
4. What are some of the positive outcomes from "roaming the wilderness"?
5. Which of the development suggestions would be most effective for me? Why?
6. Am I facing a change where I might find myself "roaming the wilderness"?

7. Am I prepared to "roam the wilderness"? If yes, in what way(s)? If no, what do I need to do?
8. Is this a skill I need to develop? If yes, select at least one of the suggestions from the above list to focus on.
9. How do I see myself using this strategy when dealing with change/transition?
10. Even if not undergoing a change or transition, how can I apply this strategy to my daily life to make it more meaningful, pleasant, and positive?

PRESER<u>V</u>ING SANITY: Vision

"What appears to be the end may really be a new beginning."
—Unknown

THE VISION STRATEGY IS the third step in William Bridges's (1991, 2004) transition process, what he calls the "new beginning." In dealing with change and transition, it is through the vision or the new beginning that everything comes together. The old or former merges with the ideas from the neutral zone or the wilderness and becomes transformed into a new identity, understanding, value, or attitude. New beginnings are linked to vision, and it is the vision that provides the direction that was lacking in the neutral zone or wilderness.

When thinking of vision, I am always reminded of the story of the seahorse going out to seek his fortune. This seahorse was wandering aimlessly through the ocean when he came upon a sea creature that asked where he was going. The seahorse responded that he was seeking his fortune. The sea creature had a pair of flippers and told the seahorse if he bought them, he would get to his fortune much faster. So the seahorse bought the flippers and he indeed did zip through the ocean faster.

He came upon another sea creature who asked where he was going. The seahorse repeated his story, and this creature, having a

26

motorized sea scooter for sale, told the seahorse that if he bought it, he would get to his fortune in no time. So the seahorse bought the scooter and was then flying through the ocean.

He came upon a shark who asked where he was going. When the seahorse told him that he was out to seek his fortune, the shark told him he knew a shortcut and then opened his mouth. The seahorse took the shortcut, never to be heard from again.

The moral of the story? If you don't know where you are going, you are liable to end up somewhere else and not even know it!

After negotiating the neutral zone/wilderness, we do need direction so that we can be successful in our new beginning. Vision provides this direction. It is the image of what we want the future to look like. The vision provides purpose and meaning and in doing so gives hope, enthusiasm, importance, and inspiration to what we hope to accomplish or what we hope to be.

When moving into my first educational administrative role, my new beginning came when I finally let go of my classroom teacher mind-set and began to think like an educational leader while not losing sight of what the classroom teacher goes through day in and day out. When I was emotionally ready to do things differently, my new beginning dawned. When I clarified the vision I had for my department and staff, with me at the helm, I was truly on my way in my new role.

What can we do to further develop the skill of handling new beginnings? This strategy of vision?

1. Articulate the vision. I like to ask workshop participants what their idea of a perfect day is. Many have to really think before they can answer. If one doesn't know what one's perfect day looks like, how will it ever be recognized or appreciated when it arrives? It is the same with vision. The vision, the direction, the goal must be clear and identifiable, and one must be able to talk about it, share what it is with

others. Use the touchstones from the relationships strategy to talk about the vision.

2. Develop a plan to reach the vision. Write down, step-by-step, how the vision can be achieved.
3. Implement the plan of action. Get involved and stay involved. Provide incentives as needed.
4. Celebrate successes when milestones have been reached in the plan's implementation. Do something that has meaning and that will feel like a reward.

Reader Reflection

1. What is vision or a new beginning?
2. Why is this strategy an important one when dealing with change/transition?
3. When would it be good to use this strategy?
4. How does vision provide direction?
5. Which of the development suggestions would be most effective for me? Why?
6. Am I facing a change where I might find myself needing vision or a new beginning?
7. Is this a skill I need to develop? If yes, select at least one of the suggestions from the above list to focus on.
8. How do I see myself using this strategy when dealing with change/transition?
9. Even if not undergoing a change or transition, how can I apply this strategy to my daily life to make it more meaningful, pleasant, and positive?

PRESERVING SANITY:
Irreverent Thinking

"Man's mind, once stretched by a new idea,
never regains its original dimensions"
—Oliver Wendell Holmes

THE STRATEGY OF IRREVERENT thinking relates to using divergent thinking or thinking that goes beyond conventional wisdom to help deal with change and transition. Dealing with the unexpected is one of the most difficult things anyone can face. The unexpected moves us out of our comfort zone before we realize what is happening. When faced with the unforeseen, traditional or logical thinking may not provide us with the best option to deal with the situation. We may be better served thinking creatively or divergently.

According to J. P. Guilford (1967), divergent thinking is the ability to draw on ideas from across disciplines to reach a deeper understanding of the world and one's place in it. This type of thinking is important when dealing with change and transition because a person can generate many unique and creative responses and solutions to deal with issues presented by a changing situation. A wonderful example of divergent thinking is how NASA staff came up with a new filtering system for the crippled Apollo 13 spacecraft using only items that were available on the vehicle, none of which were originally designed to become a filtering system.

Oliver Wendell Holmes Jr. said, "Man's mind, once stretched by a new idea, never regains its original dimensions." This is not a bad philosophy for helping us deal with change. Change often requires us to find new comfort zones; it doesn't always permit us to return to our "original spot." If we can come up with new and different ideas to cope with our new situation, our new spot, our "new dimension," we will be that much further ahead in responding to change and transition.

Divergent thinking means marching to the beat of a different drummer. Following the crowd isn't always the best strategy when dealing with change. The best visual for this is a cartoon in which lemmings are running toward a body of water and certain death, except for one lemming who has an inner tube wrapped around him. He can be viewed as a divergent thinker, one who assessed the situation and came up with a unique solution to his predicament.

How can be we like the lemming with the inner tube or the NASA staff? What techniques can be used to develop the strategy of divergent thinking?

1. Brainstorm ideas. This is where ideas are spontaneously generated in response to a problem, issue, or situation. Ideas can then be sorted and categorized.
2. Ask, "What if?" Take the situation at hand and make a list of what-if questions.
3. Create a mind map. This is a diagram that visually outlines thoughts. A single word is placed in the center (such as moving across country) and feelings, thoughts, ideas, and ways to deal with this situation are written as offshoots from the center. This is a nice way to organize and summarize thoughts. Sometimes, the solution to an issue clearly emerges from this process.

4. Journal. Anyone who has kept a diary is familiar with journaling. A journal is a means to record thoughts and ideas. Capturing thoughts at the time they are bouncing in one's head and then reading them later may lead one to discover a hidden solution to an issue. Getting the thoughts down in writing may also have a calming effect, especially when the change is inducing moments of stress. When my mom was dying, I did journal my thoughts and found it to be very cathartic.

Reader Reflection

1. What is irreverent thinking?
2. Why is it important to not always follow the crowd when dealing with change?
3. Why is this strategy an important one when dealing with change/transition?
4. When would it be good to use this strategy?
5. Which of the development suggestions would be most effective for me? Why?
6. Am I facing a change where I might find myself needing to think irreverently?
7. Is this a skill I need to develop? If yes, select at least one of the suggestions from the above list to focus on.
8. How do I see myself using this strategy when dealing with change/transition?
9. Even if not undergoing a change or transition, how can I apply this strategy to my daily life to make it more meaningful, pleasant, and positive?

PRESERVI**N**G SANITY:
Negotiating Roadblocks

"If the boulders are moved, even a river will change its course."
—Unknown

NEGOTIATING ROADBLOCKS IS A strategy that focuses on the ability to change course and direction when change and transition place obstacles in the way of life's journey. Marsha Sinetar has said, "Life's ups and downs provide windows of opportunities to determine your values and goals—Think of using all obstacles as stepping stones to build the life you want" (Sinetar 2013).

Why is dealing with roadblocks important when dealing with change? When in the midst of change or transitions, life is like a roller-coaster ride; it is full of ups and downs. But as Sinetar says, these ups and downs offer us opportunities, chances to determine what is important and what direction we really want to take. That move out of our comfort zone forces us to reevaluate ourselves, to search for pockets of strength we didn't even know we had, and to move onward and upward to where we want to be. All roadblocks and obstacles present unique challenges to us, but within those challenges are wonderful opportunities to further develop our skills, experiences, knowledge, networks, relationships, and ourselves in general.

I would like to highlight this with another example from my personal life. As mentioned in the introduction, I was very involved with the College Reading and Learning Association (CRLA). As president-elect of the organization, I had the privilege of planning the 1992 annual conference, which happened to be the association's twenty-fifth annual conference. My conference theme was "Celebrating the Diversity in Teaching and Learning," and because it was a milestone anniversary conference, I wanted a memorable keynote speaker. I was most fortunate to get Alex Haley, who is probably most remembered for *Roots*.

I was working in Salem, Oregon, at the time I was planning the conference. One of the phone calls I received on February 10, 1992, was from a Seattle, Washington, colleague asking how I was doing. I responded that I was busy but fine. The person sounded incredulous and asked how I could be fine (and sound so calm) at a time like this. I had no clue about what my colleague was talking, so I asked what was going on. My colleague, another CRLA member, had called to talk to me about breaking news: Alex Haley had just died. What was I going to do about the conference?

My conference was scheduled to begin on April 9, and Haley passed away on February 10. Talk about change happening unexpectedly. Indeed, it had. Talk about a roadblock being placed in one's path. I had one big time!

After hanging up the phone, I sat in stunned silence for a few moments. After my brief period of mourning both the loss of a great writer as well as the loss of my keynote speaker, I shifted my mind-set to viewing this as an opportunity and went about retooling the conference and the keynote speaker. I must admit that I derived some inspiration for my retooling efforts from *The Wizard of Oz*.

The book's characters are my favorite examples of those who refuse to let roadblocks keep them from their goal. No matter what was put in their way of reaching Oz or their goal of returning home, they rose to the challenge (often using their creativity) and overcame the roadblock. They truly used all obstacles as stepping-stones to get to what they wanted.

How does one develop the skill of negotiating roadblocks, of viewing obstacles as stepping-stones, and successfully using them to reach goals?

1. Identify what is standing in the way of reaching the goal. Is it emotion based (fear, anger, doubt, worry, sadness)? Is it something physical (distance, lack of a resource)? Is it health related (physical ailment, weight issue, lack of exercise)? Is it our mind-set (resistance to the change, negativity, my way is the only way)?

2. Determine the best approach to overcoming the obstacle. Does the issue require just taking a step back, slowing down a bit, and cooling off? Do you feel hampered as if in a straitjacket where the connections must be determined before the bounds can be loosened or severed? Is the challenge more of a hurdle for which you need to gain momentum to jump over it? Has something impassable like a boulder been dropped on the path where a whole new route must be found? Is it just the "yellow light" flashing indicating to us the need to slow down and use caution? Does it feel like the wall has been hit? As Michael Jordan says, "Obstacles don't have to stop you. If you run into a wall, don't turn around and give up. Figure out how to climb it, go through it, or work around it" (Jordan 2013).

3. Blast the roadblock into manageable pieces. Break down into smaller, more manageable ways/steps the approach to overcoming the roadblock. Taking baby steps will help prevent one from becoming overwhelmed by the roadblock.

4. Be persistent. Keep on going no matter what. (Refer to suggestions presented in the chapter on persistence.)

5. Take an emotional time-out. When roadblocks are placed in our path, it is common to get flustered and react in an emotional way. This type of reaction isn't usually productive. It may be cathartic, but it isn't going to remove the roadblock. When facing the roadblock, we must begin to look at it with our logic and reason lenses. This will help identify the relevance of the roadblock and the means by which to overcome it.

6. Take a view from a different perspective. View the roadblock from someone else's perspective (spouse, child, coworker, boss, friend, sibling, or parent). Try to see it inside out and upside down. Is it truly what we think, or have we misunderstand the situation? Am I clearly seeing the picture, or are there clouds or fog in the way? Have others dealt with the same obstacle? How did they overcome it? Have I made assumptions about the issue? Do these assumptions help to remove the roadblock, or do they make it worse?

7. Think irreverently, divergently, creatively. Go beyond conventional wisdom. (Refer to suggestions in the chapter on irreverent thinking.)

8. Use the touchstones to talk through the situation. Talking to others will help put or keep things in perspective. Other people may have similar experiences and may be able to share how they dealt with the roadblock. In addition to the touchstones, seek expert help when the obstacle seems insurmountable and the desire to give up is strong.

9. Be action oriented. Change overwhelms us. The roadblocks within the change can stop us in our track. This is the time to take a deep breath and step into action. Focus on the following: Just what is the roadblock? The circumstance? Can

I handle it? Can I control it? What parts can't I control? How do I gain the upper hand with this? How can I influence this circumstance? What resources do I need?

10. Think like a winner. Believing roadblocks can be overcome is half the battle. Have confidence. Steer clear from doubts because they will only immobilize any effort. Self-doubts also turn attention away from solutions and keep the attention on the problem. The calmer one can be, the clearer the mind and the better one is able to think divergently and creatively about the issue(s). Winners don't quit; they rise above to meet the challenge head-on.

Reader Reflection

1. What does it mean to negotiate roadblocks?
2. Roadblocks present challenges, but often, opportunities arise from challenges. What does this mean? Give some examples of opportunities arising in this way.
3. Why is this strategy an important one when dealing with change/transition?
4. When would it be good to use this strategy?
5. Which of the development suggestions would be most effective for me? Why?
6. Am I facing a change where I might find myself needing to negotiate the roadblocks?
7. Is this a skill I need to develop? If yes, select at least one of the suggestions from the above list to focus on.
8. How do I see myself using this strategy when dealing with change/transition?
9. Even if not undergoing a change or transition, how can I apply this strategy to my daily life to make it more meaningful, pleasant, and positive?

PRESERVIN<u>G</u>
SANITY: Giggling

"If you truly want to improve your life, laugh at
least once more today than yesterday."
—Unknown

GIGGLING IS A FORM of laughter. Laughter is an involuntary reaction
to something one finds humorous (stories, jokes, thoughts) or
to something physical, such as being tickled. Giggling is a visual
expression of positive emotions, such as happiness, joy, and relief.

The relief theory provides one explanation for laughter, and
Sigmund Freud (1928) in this theory indicated that laughter releases
tension and "psychic energy." Giggling (laughter) is a strategy for
dealing with change, because changes and transitions do create
tension and stress in our lives that, if not relieved, can have detrimental
effects on us. We have talked about change moving us away from our
comfort zone. When this happens, we can feel threatened and the
balance in our life is now out of sync. Stress and tension are normal
responses to this. We have also talked about transitions, which are
the emotional or psychological component of the change process.
Internal stressors associated with transitions can be the inability to

accept the uncertainty of the change, unrealistic expectations with regard to the change, negative self-talk, and being pessimistic.

Giggling is a strategy that helps counteract the effects stress and tension have on our bodies. In addition to making life more enjoyable in general, giggling (laugher) has been proven beneficial for one's health (Mayo Clinic Staff 2011). Laughter creates physical changes in one's body, such as the following:

1. Enhancing the intake of oxygen-rich air, which stimulates one's heart, lungs, and muscles (In addition, it increases the endorphins that are released by the brain.)
2. Producing a good, relaxed feeling in the body by relieving one's stress response
3. Stimulating circulation and aiding muscle relaxation, which helps reduce some physical symptoms of stress
4. Improving one's immune system through the release of neuropeptides that help fight stress as a result of the positive thoughts/laughter
5. Relieving pain by causing the body to produce natural painkillers (endorphins)

Change and transition can make situations difficult for many. Giggling can make it easier to cope with difficult situations. It also has a way of bringing people together. It can strengthen relationships, enhance teamwork, and help diffuse conflict.

How else can giggling help in dealing with change? Giggling and laughter give one the courage and strength to find sources of meaning and hope in the changed environment. Feelings of anxiety, anger, and sadness aren't making appearances when one is laughing. As a result, one is able to stay more focused on dealing with the change and perhaps view the situation or issue more realistically. Sensations of threat from being ousted from the comfort zone can be diminished through laughter. A phrase from a perpetual calendar sums up the importance of laughter: if you truly want to improve your life, laugh at least once more today than yesterday.

If giggling and laughter seem to be missing from life because the stress and tension that have accompanied change and transition make it difficult, what can we do to develop this skill, this strategy?

1. Find or create opportunities to giggle. Watch a funny movie or television show. Read the comics. Share a good joke or funny story. Check out the local bookstore's humor section. Play with a pet. Do something silly (like buying children's bubbles and blowing them in the wind or spraying silly string). Play with young children.

2. Share laughter with your touchstone and other friends. Do fun activities together. Play board games.

3. Smile. A smile is the start of a giggle or laughter. And it is said that smiles are contagious. Others may join you in a "smile fest."

4. Develop the ability to laugh at yourself. Share your embarrassing moments. A perfect example of this comes from my own life. When I was in ninth grade, I was part of my school's team on the Pittsburgh, Pennsylvania, television show *Junior High Quiz*. Questions were posed by moderator Ricki Wertz, and the sooner one hit the buzzer and responded with a correct answer, the higher the points scored. The score clock was ticking away after the question, "What are the four taste sensations?" I kept telling myself that I did, indeed, know the answer to this, so I eventually hit the buzzer. I proudly responded, "Hot, cold, good, and bad." Ms. Wertz paused for a moment before announcing that that was not correct. (The correct answer is sweet, sour, salty, and bitter.) I don't know what was worse: watching the show on television and reliving the moment or going to

school on Monday morning after the show aired and being teased by my classmates. Or having the lesson in my home economics class that Monday on that very subject. I did survive this situation by making a joke of it and laughing at myself. And by laughing at myself first, people were eventually laughing *with* me and not *at* me.

5. Develop a giggle bulletin board. Make space on the refrigerator, a wall, the side of a file cabinet, or wherever there is space in the house or the office. Post comics, signs, funny sayings, bumper stickers, or anything that will make you giggle, laugh, or bring about a smile.

6. Use children as role models. (Children were introduced as models of enthusiasm in the chapter on that strategy. Refer also to the information in that chapter.) Children are experts on laughing, having fun, playing, and not taking things too seriously.

Reader Reflection

1. What is giggling?
2. What is laughter?
3. What do giggling and laughter do for us?
4. What physical changes does laughter create in one's body?
5. Why is this strategy an important one when dealing with change/transition?
6. When would it be good to use this strategy?
7. Which of the development suggestions would be most effective for me? Why?
8. Am I facing a change where I might find myself needing to giggle more?
9. Is this a skill I need to develop? If yes, select at least one of the suggestions from the above list to focus on.

10. How do I see myself using this strategy when dealing with change/transition?
11. Even if not undergoing a change or transition, how can I apply this strategy to my daily life to make it more meaningful, pleasant, and positive?

PRESERVING SANITY:
Savoring Mistakes

"If you want to succeed, double your failure rate."
—Thomas Watson

A MISTAKE IS AN error, something in a piece of work or in a decision that is incorrect. A mistake can also be a misunderstanding of something. Usually, mistakes are unintentional. The strategy of savoring mistakes is about adopting an attitude that mistakes are learning opportunities. Mistakes teach us. They are nothing more than an adjustment to the original plan.

When change and transition are upon us, we often have to make decisions about the new environment or the direction we need to take to effectively deal with the change. Depending on the situation, our state of mind, and the information available when we are making these decisions, it is not uncommon to see lots and lots of mistakes being made. And if our role in the changed situation has us performing unfamiliar tasks, look out! Mistakes are bound to happen.

This strategy offers us a new way of looking at mistakes. Instead of feeling as if they are something "bad," failures, or more obstacles in the changed environment, we need to instead view them as opportunities for growth and learning. Mistakes are actually good for us. They do show us things that need more attention.

Thomas Edison said, "I haven't failed. I've found 10,000 ways that don't work" (Edison 2013). Edison was inspired by his mistakes; they encouraged him to work harder to find solutions for his work. If Edison hadn't savored his mistakes, he would not have invented the light bulb. As he said, "We now know a thousand ways not to build a light bulb" (Edison 2013).

Life is about choices and even more so when dealing with change. Choices mean decisions. If the decision is right and works well, things will continue to progress. If the decision is wrong, look for the lesson in it. Reevaluate, and try again. As long as we are learning from our mistakes (and don't make the same mistake over and over again), we will continue to move forward.

In my professional life, I quickly learned the value of mistakes. While working at Blue Mountain Community College in Pendleton, Oregon, I developed a book titled *Challenging Adults to Read Effectively*. The book quickly became known as the CARE manual, and I was asked to share it at several professional conferences throughout the Pacific Northwest. This was my first venture in the public speaking arena (and that was a big change for me professionally). I prepared a presentation and had delivered it at several adult learner-focused conferences. These audiences found the CARE manual to be most helpful, and I was pleased with the response. I was on the program at an International Reading Association conference in Moscow, Idaho. My audience, however, had no adult educators in it. The room was full of high school principals, district superintendents, and a few reading specialists. I started what in the past had been a very successful presentation. Not so at this conference.

People got up and walked out of the room. Most of those that remained looked at me impassively or with eyes glazed over. My mistake was not knowing my audience and their needs and not being able to adapt the content of my presentation to the needs of the participants. I was glad I was in Moscow, Idaho, because I didn't think word would spread from there to Portland, Oregon, or Seattle, Washington, about what a horrible speaker I was.

I did learn to have adaptations of my presentations ready so that I could quickly switch gears depending on my audience. Had it not been for my Moscow mistake and turning that into a learning opportunity, I may never have gone on to further develop my public speaking skills. Mistakes are truly good for us. They help mold us and make us who we are. And like the Idaho experience was for me, mistakes often become valuable assets to and for us.

How else can mistakes help us deal with change and transition? They are an indication of our willingness to try new things. Trying new things is a sign of growth and improvement. Scott Berkun, a former Microsoft employee and author of *Making Things Happen* feels that mistakes are also a way for us to acknowledge reality (2005). He states, "If you can't see the gaps, flaws, or weaknesses in your behavior you're forever trapped in the same behavior and limitations you've always had, possibly since you were a child."

What are the keys to developing this strategy of savoring mistakes?

1. Adopt a new philosophy toward mistakes. Instead of viewing them as something bad, do consider them as gifts of learning or pearls of wisdom. Look at mistakes as blessings. Karen Salmansohn (2013) has coined a new word: blesson. According to her, "It's when you're able to view painful lessons as blessings. A blesson is what happens when you see the blessing in the lesson that your challenge taught you." Think about how young children deal with mistakes. They simply ask for a do-over and move on.

2. Acknowledge mistakes and accept responsibility for them. Avoid placing blame, especially on someone else.

3. Look for the lesson in each mistake. Assess what happened. Think about what can be done differently if in a similar situation or faced with a similar decision. Determine if there were actually any advantages or benefits with this mistake.

4. Share with someone (your touchstone) what happened. Talk about the mistake with someone. Perhaps they've done something similar and can share their experience, how they coped, and what they learned.

5. Learn to giggle/laugh about what happened. While whatever happened may not be funny at the time, upon reflection, there is probably something humorous that can be gleaned from the situation or decision. We are usually embarrassed by our mistakes, which can elevate our feelings of stress and tension. (Remember that giggling and laughing are stress reducers.)

Reader Reflection

1. What is a mistake?
2. On what does the strategy of savoring mistakes focus?
3. In this strategy, mistakes are not viewed as something "bad." What is the perspective of mistakes in this strategy?
4. What is a "blesson"? How can a blesson help in dealing with mistakes?
5. Why is this strategy an important one when dealing with change/transition?
6. When would it be good to use this strategy?
7. Which of the development suggestions would be most effective for me? Why?
8. Am I facing a change where I might find myself needing to savor mistakes?
9. Is this a skill I need to develop? If yes, select at least one of the suggestions from the above list to focus on.

10. How do I see myself using this strategy when dealing with change/transition?

11. Even if not undergoing a change or transition, how can I apply this strategy to my daily life to make it more meaningful, pleasant, and positive?

PRESERVING S<u>A</u>NITY:
Atta Persons

"Kindness is more than deeds. It is an attitude, an expression,
a look, a touch. It is anything that lifts another person."
—Unknown

THE ONE THING THAT change and transition can do is mess with our sense of who we are and how we feel about ourselves. Not being in our comfort zone, dealing with the chaos that can surround the change, and with having to do new tasks or step into a new role, it is easy to get down on ourselves about a lot of stuff. This strategy of "atta persons" focuses on the need to let those around us know that they are appreciated as well as to give ourselves the occasional pat on the back.

Appreciation should be the heart and the core of all relationships. This is so important in times of change and transition, especially when that change and transition is creating much stress and tension for all involved. Never is it more important to feel valued, to feel important, or to feel recognized.

When the world around us shifts, as it can when we undergo change and transition, and we are doing our best to just get along, tackle the new technology at work, deal with the changing attitude of the new teenager in the house, or adjust to the new house and community, a little appreciation would go a long way. It would make us feel good. Appreciation, through words of praise or encouragement, has a motivating effect on us. Those kind words or deeds have a way of strengthening the bonds between people.

Working through changes or transitions can be physically and mentally tiring. However, a kind word that shows someone else has noticed the effort or the work truly goes a long way. Personally, I become eager to do more or to do it better when others notice what I am doing. Just the fact that someone noticed lets me know what I am doing matters and makes a difference.

When I shifted into an administrative role, I worked with support staff and supervised faculty. I made it a point to regularly let them know what I felt about the work they were doing. Appreciation and recognition of their work came weekly rather than just one day a year (like Administrative Assistant Day) or one week a year (Teacher Appreciation Week). I left "butterfly" notes regularly. These might say, "Have I told you lately how much I appreciate all you do?" or "Wishing you a super day and a pleasant week. You are special!" Smiles, nods, words of encouragement, and words of appreciation were a part of this weekly routine. Whether what they did was big or small, part of the job or self-initiated, for a student or for a colleague, I was committed to making sure the faculty and staff in my department knew they were valued and what they did was important.

It is vital that any "atta person" comes from the heart and is delivered in a sincere and genuine way. If not, the words or actions become meaningless. Recognizing and appreciating others doesn't have to be anything elaborate. Gifts, flowers, candy, food, whatever—it all has its place. But most people just want to hear, "You did a great job," "You look terrific," "Thank you for noticing," or "Your comment made me feel great!" It is the message that is shared that matters the most.

Recognizing others, valuing them, and showing appreciation has a profound impact on the lives of others, but it also has a positive health benefit for the person who delivers the "atta person." Research (Benson 1975; Luks 2001) shows that being kind to others not only makes the person who does the kind act feel good, but being kind has a significant physical and mental health benefit.

Dr. Herbert Benson, a Harvard cardiologist who has been involved in scientific research for more than thirty years, tells us that when we help others, it allows us to "forget one's self." When we carry out an act of kindness or give an "atta person," our body rewards us by creating a feel-good sensation, which boosts self-esteem and well-being. This sensation is triggered when the body manufactures chemicals called endorphins. These endorphins are naturally occurring morphine-like substances that create a feeling of bliss within us. In addition to creating a feel-good experience, they also help to reduce the intensity of any pain messages being sent to the brain.

When the process of change is triggering stress and tension or sending pain messages to the brain, receiving an "atta person" can have a calming effect. Likewise, giving someone an "atta person" can help diminish some of the stress symptoms as well as provide a natural high. The implementation of this strategy is a win-win for all involved.

There is a Cherokee story of a battle between the "two wolves" inside us all. One "wolf" is considered evil, as it represents, among other things, anger, envy, jealously false pride, superiority, regret, and self-pity. The other "wolf" is considered good as it represents, among other things, benevolence, empathy, compassion, love, hope, joy, and kindness. The "wolf" that wins the battle is the one we feed. This strategy of "atta persons" focuses on us feeding the "good wolf" so that in times of change, we are able to project those positive and good qualities, making ourselves and those around us feel better about what is happening while undergoing change and transition.

So how do we go about "feeding the good wolf"? How do we develop this skill, this strategy of "atta persons"?

1. Cultivate the mind-set of always looking out for the good in someone or something. Showing appreciation becomes easy and almost second nature, if it comes naturally.
2. Maintain an optimistic outlook about things; have a positive orientation. Smile a lot!
3. Have a kind attitude. Kindness as an attitude is infectious. When you're willing to share your kindness, others will be inspired by your example and think about doing something as kind themselves. Fan that flame by being kind to everyone.
4. Set a goal to give out at least one "atta person" per day. Let a family member know how their comment, smile, or deed made a difference. Boost a colleague with a kind word. When a stranger holds the door open, make sure to thank him/her. When someone says, "Thank you," make sure the response is "You're welcome."
5. Send an "atta person" to someone (the more personal, the better). While e-mail, tweets, and use of social media have their place, words of appreciation delivered that way may feel too impersonal to some, especially if a general e-blast is going to many. If sharing a compliment in this way, try to avoid e-blasts. Send cards and notes. Send a symbol, like a blue ribbon or a gold medal (can be one printed on paper) with a comment on what is being recognized (e.g., "I noticed your son won the spelling bee. Congrats.")
6. Be observant. We don't know what others may be facing in their personal or professional lives. Watch for opportunities to bring a smile to someone's face. I have noticed parents with young children in long lines where the children get impatient. When I can, I will say to the parent, "I admire your patience with your children. I know they would rather be somewhere

else playing, so please go ahead of me in this line." Talk about making someone's day. The thank-you from the parent and the smiles on the children's faces are enough to let me know that I had made a difference for them.

7. Phone someone who hasn't been in touch for a while and just let them know that they've been in your thoughts and prayers.

8. Be generous with compliments.

9. Lend a helping hand when needed. Offer to watch someone's children to give them a break. Walk someone's pet. Prepare a meal for someone so they won't have to after a long day at work or after dealing with issues that change and transition present them.

10. Just listen. There are times when just lending an ear to someone is the best way to show appreciation and compassion. The nature of the conversation will determine follow-up comments or questions.

11. Get creative. Make a list with at least seven ways you can give someone an "atta person." Commit to taking a week and give out at least one "atta person" a day.

Reader Reflection

1. What is an "atta person"?
2. On what does the strategy "atta persons" focus?
3. Why is this strategy an important one when dealing with change/transition?
4. What physical benefits might I receive from giving "atta persons"?
5. When would it be good to use this strategy?
6. Which of the development suggestions would be most effective for me? Why?
7. Am I facing a change where I might find myself needing to receive or give "atta persons"?

8. Is this a skill I need to develop? If yes, select at least one of the suggestions from the above list to focus on.

9. How do I see myself using this strategy when dealing with change/transition?

10. Even if not undergoing a change or transition, how can I apply this strategy to my daily life to make it more meaningful, pleasant, and positive?

PRESERVING SA**N**ITY:
New Style of Thinking

"We can't solve problems by using the same kind of
thinking we used when we created them."
—Albert Einstein

WHEN CHANGE AND TRANSITION happen, something becomes
different. Sometimes, the differences are minor and present no
need to alter the way of doing things or thinking (e.g., someone
repaints a room in their home). Sometimes, the differences are
major (car breaks down and needs a costly repair), causing us to
make a quick decision that could have a long-term effect on family,
budget, transportation needs, etc. And, other times, the differences
are seismic (finding one suddenly single or finding one out of a job),
creating the need to overhaul how things are done, how one thinks,
or how decisions are made. When we are in the midst of an overhaul
or decision making that may have a long-term effect, doing so with
the old way of thinking may not result in a satisfactory outcome.
Albert Einstein said, "The definition of insanity is doing the same
thing over and over and expecting different results" (Einstein
2013). So in an overhaul or a quick-decision situation, a new style

of thinking may be required to prevent us from appearing (or going) insane.

The strategy of new style of thinking presents a method of decision making that goes beyond the conventional—the "same old, same old." Please note that there is nothing wrong with conventional ways of doing things or making decisions when in a status quo situation. But when faced with changes and transitions that present major differences, what worked in the old may not work in the new. In a changed environment, when we start getting down on ourselves because things just aren't working out, they may not be working out because we are doing what Anthony Robbins indicates: "If you do what you've always done, you'll get what you've always gotten" (Robbins 2013).

Losing weight may be a goal, but eating and exercise habits remain the same. Saving money is a goal, but style of spending remains the same. Trimming the budget at work is desired, but staffing and services don't change. Demands at work are increasing, but there are still only twenty-four hours in a day. In these situations, we are not going to get desired results by perpetuating the "same" or by just working harder. We must work and think smarter; work and think differently.

Lagace (2001), in her essay that summarizes three essays that address compelling leadership issues, talks of Rosabeth Moss Kanter nominating the kaleidoscope as a symbol companies should use for the global information era. According to her, it symbolized ever-changing patterns and endless new possibilities, both of which are guided by the human imagination. Kanter's kaleidoscopic thinking provides a wonderful model for a new style of thinking and approaching decision making differently, especially when dealing with change or needing to create change. She says, "Creativity is a lot like looking at the world through a kaleidoscope. You look at a set of elements, the same ones everyone else sees, but then reassemble those floating bits and pieces into an enticing new possibility" (Kanter 2013). The notion of forming new patterns from existing information or resources is so simple yet something we might not normally consider doing.

Viewing things from a new angle is important when attempting to successfully navigate the seas of change. Remember that if we want the end result to be different, our actions and decisions must also be different. However, the difference may come about by doing something as simple as tweaking what we already have. One time, I was trying to reorganize items under the kitchen sink to better use the space. I wanted to put plastic grocery bags in a storage unit drawer, but the unit took up too much space when I placed its bottom on. However, when I turned it on its side, it fit beautifully.

How does one go about developing a new style of thinking?

1. Practice kaleidoscopic thinking. Take all the pieces for the situation (write out the pieces on index cards) and play with arranging them in different configurations.

2. Put on the critical thinking cap. When one thinks critically, the situation is analytically evaluated. This helps with bringing out different points of view related to the situation. Challenge and analyze what the motivation for doing something is, what thought processes are being used in the decision making, and what conclusions are being derived. Use reflection throughout the analysis. Ask, "Could I be wrong? What assumptions am I making? Are the assumptions correct? Are there other explanations? Other perspectives? Other viewpoints?" Seek out evidence to support ideas, beliefs, and conclusions.

3. Use the "challenge card." Reflect on the points of view, statements, claims, and arguments. Can weaknesses in each be identified? If so, what does that do to the situation? Are other explanations possible?

4. Practice "parachute thinking." Parachutes only work when they are open. In using a new style of thinking, keep an open mind and be willing to change it based on the evidence. Ask what it would take to create a mind-set change.

5. Gain a fresh perspective. Visit someone or someplace to experience something different from the norm. This may provide new ideas or a way of taking the "kaleidoscopic piece" of one's life and helping with the rearrangement. Talk to someone who has a totally different point of view on the issue or situation. Think of the story of the blind men and the elephant. Depending on what part of the elephant was touched, the perspective on what the elephant was like differed. Look at the pieces of the situation in this manner to help gain other perspectives.

Reader Reflection

1. What is a key issue with thinking in "old ways" when dealing with change/transition?
2. What is the focus of the new style of thinking strategy?
3. What is the theory of kaleidoscopic thinking?
4. Why does the theory of kaleidoscopic thinking provide a good model for a new style of thinking?
5. Why is this strategy an important one when dealing with change/transition?
6. When would it be good to use this strategy?
7. Which of the development suggestions would be most effective for me? Why?
8. Am I facing a change where I might find myself needing to practice a new style of thinking?
9. Is this a skill I need to develop? If yes, select at least one of the suggestions from the above list to focus on.

10. How do I see myself using this strategy when dealing with change/transition?
11. Even if not undergoing a change or transition, how can I apply this strategy to my daily life to make it more meaningful, pleasant, and positive?

PRESERVING SAN_ITY:
Innovativeness

"Allow your vision to know no boundaries."
—Unknown

WHEN CHANGE AND TRANSITION are upon us, I can't stress enough the importance of thinking differently, of using novel approaches to deal with and face what the change or transition presents. Because how we think and approach the change is so vital, this strategy presents yet another way of thinking. It is similar to irreverent thinking and a new style of thinking but provides a slightly different twist giving yet another way to stay sane and positive amid the change.

By definition, an innovation is the introduction of something new (idea, method, process, service, product, or device) that allows one to do something different. There are many lists of notable innovators. My personal list includes Christiann Barnard, Florence Nightingale, and Alexander Fleming for influencing the world of medicine; Archimedes, Marie Curie, Albert Einstein, and the Wright Brothers for altering the direction of science; Bill Gates, Steve Jobs, and Mark Zuckerberg for revolutionizing technology; and Alexander Graham Bell, Thomas Edison, Benjamin Franklin, and Henry Ford for transforming the status quo. So what does all this have to do with change and transition? Just as those on my personal list of innovators had to look at common items and see something different, so must we if the expectation is to positively and successfully survive the changes and transitions that we encounter.

Innovativeness requires us to think across borders and through boundaries, as Kanter offers in her essay on leadership (Lagace 2001). Innovativeness is a way of thinking that questions and challenges prevailing thought and opens us up to numerous solutions rather than just the way something has always been done. Innovativeness permits us to exceed our own expectations. When we are innovative, we are creative. When we are creative, we think outside the box; we use our imagination. Thinking or acting in an innovative way and with a purpose may be just what it takes to propel us through the change and its transitions to a new beginning.

The nine-dot puzzle (the challenge is to connect the dots by drawing four straight, continuous lines through each of the nine dots without lifting the pencil) is frequently used to demonstrate the need to think outside the box. One of the many solutions to the puzzle is to go beyond the boundaries of the area created by the nine dots to link all dots in four straight, continuous lines.

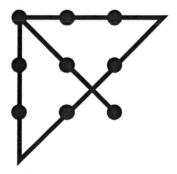

This is an example of one solution to the nine-dot puzzle,
showing how one must go outside the boundaries
of the dots to successfully solve the puzzle.

I tried to use out-of-the-box thinking when I was a classroom teacher. Once when teaching a middle school math class to a group of special education students (I was giving coming attractions on what was next in math), everyone moaned and groaned when I mentioned fractions. "They're hard," I would hear. Others offered, "I've never been able to understand fractions." So one day, during a language arts class, I had the students read a recipe and make the candy. I made sure one group halved the ingredients and another decreased their recipe by a quarter. While the students indulged in their final products, I did a lesson summary and announced that they had just used fractions to make their candy. "No way," I heard. "That was easy." Indeed, I told them, fractions are easy once we know the trick to handling them. By providing the class with a creative activity, it took no time for their preconceived notions and fears about fractions to fade away.

Thinking creatively and innovatively allows us to overcome the fear we might experience with the change/transition. Being innovative also helps us avoid getting into a rut with our thinking; it helps create a new routine with our way of thinking about and approaching what faces us. If you really want to be successful in the changed environment, you must change the routine way of doing things so that the results are different and meet the desire needs or goals.

This strategy of innovativeness also helps us deal with change and transition, because it challenges us to put aside comfortable habits and try something new (both of which are vital to remain sane and positive in times of change and transition). The shift from our comfort zone may have us falling back and relying on old habits rather than trying something new.

In conducting workshops on change, I frequently have participants do an activity that illustrates how habits interfere with listening. For example, I might say, "Papa Bull, Mama Bull, and Baby Bull are out in the pasture. Baby Bull gets hurt. Who does Baby Bull run to for help?"

Most will answer, "Mama Bull," coming from a stereotypical view and a traditional habit of thinking that children will first run to their moms for help. What they fail to realize is there are no female bulls, so Baby Bull would run to Papa Bull (Bianchi et al. 1990).

I can spot creative thinkers when I place five lines on the board (_____ _____ _____ _____ _____) and ask participants to write the word *think* in the spaces. Those thinking traditionally will respond with t h i n k. The creative thinkers will respond with ____t____h____i____n____k or will write the letters above or below the spaces (Bianchi et al. 1990).

How can we cultivate this strategy, this skill of innovativeness?

1. Practice out-of-the-box thinking. Remove mind-created boundaries and borders by getting rid of assumptions and restrictions. Be open to new ideas and solutions; avoid habitual thinking.
2. Practice seeing things differently. A cloud is just a cloud is just a cloud. Not so. Really look at clouds. There are so many different shapes and figures. I frequently can see dragons, dinosaurs, faces, and flowers. Cloud art is a great way to get one's mind to think differently about things. After "floating in the clouds" for a while, return to reality and apply the technique to the situation at hand.
3. Develop a list of creative uses for common things. Take an object and think of all the potential uses for it: traditional, standard, absurd, silly. For example, ice cube trays can also be used to organize jewelry, office supplies, small Christmas ornaments, and small items. (An egg carton can serve the same purpose.) Muffin tins can become a caddy for crafts, sewing, or other small items. Think about gift boxes. They can also be used as pull-out "drawers" in deep cupboards; small boxes can be used to store paper clips, pencils, etc. They also double as cupcake carriers (cut crosses into the box lid

or bottom). This is a wonderful activity to get the creative juices flowing.

4. Stretch the imagination. Take something common, and as in #3 above, brainstorm unusual uses for the item. For example, in Meadville, Pennsylvania, traffic signs have been recycled into works of art. Flower gardens have been created out of stop, yield, and other signs.

5. Establish a "creative corner." The more relaxed we are, the easier it is for our creative and innovative thoughts to flow. Establish places or activities where the daily stressors can be put at bay so ideas can rise to the surface.

6. Have a sounding board. Here's another way touchstones can be of help. Talk through ideas that address the issue or situation. Throw out one idea and ask the touchstone to add something to it. Remember Drew Carey's show *Whose Line Is It Anyway?* They did routines where someone would begin a story, and when a sound was made, that person stopped talking and the next person would have to continue the story. A similar technique will work wonders for generating creative ideas.

7. Ask a young child for suggestions. In the chapter on enthusiasm, we talked about young children at play as role models for unbridled enthusiasm. Children are naturally unconventional thinkers. When trying to be innovative, young children's take on an issue (presented to them in a way they would understand) might provide a spark of creativity that provides just what is needed for the issue at hand.

8. Flip-flop. Change the orientation of the issue or its components. Turn things around. Turn things upside down. Work backward from the desired solution or goal to what it might take to reach it. Think about what the issue might look

like if the least important outcome were the most important. What would then be the solution?

Reader Reflection

1. What is an innovation?
2. What is innovativeness?
3. What does it mean to think outside the box?
4. How might being innovative in thinking help me avoid getting into a rut with my thinking?
5. What effect do our habits have on our thinking? Do I have habits that interfere with my creative thinking?
6. Why is this strategy an important one when dealing with change/transition?
7. When would it be good to use this strategy?
8. Which of the development suggestions would be most effective for me? Why?
9. Am I facing a change where I might find myself needing to practice innovativeness in thinking?
10. Is this a skill I need to develop? If yes, select at least one of the suggestions from the above list to focus on.
11. How do I see myself using this strategy when dealing with change/transition?
12. Even if not undergoing a change or transition, how can I apply this strategy to my daily life to make it more meaningful, pleasant, and positive?

PRESERVING SANITY:
Taking Risks

"Only those who will risk going too far can
possibly find out how far one can go."
—T. S. Eliot

IN THE CONTEXT OF dealing with change and transition, taking risks
involves doing something that helps achieve a desired solution but
there is a lack of certainty about the outcome and/or a fear of failure.
When change and transition alter the course of one's journey and a
new route must be tried, there is a certain amount of risk involved
when traveling down the unknown route. However, some say a turtle
only advances by sticking its neck out. So it is with us. We must
"stick our neck out"; we must take some risks to make the necessary
adjustments in the altered environment and move forward.

A good example of risk takers is the early explorers. When all
believed the world was flat, Christopher Columbus set out to prove
them wrong. He had to have the courage to lose sight of the shore
in order to discover new horizons. (Think he was moved out of his
comfort zone?) It is the same with us when dealing with the aftermath
of change. We have to have the courage to lose sight of what was in

order to become what will be. The first of the three stages of transition is when something ends. We definitely give up all or part of what was. The familiar is gone. Uncertainty about what will follow replaces what had been our norm. And the second stage of the transition is the wilderness or the neutral zone where uncertainty rules.

While we may be able to guide where we want to go or what we want to do in the changed environment, we aren't able to control the outcome. All we can do is plan what we want. In planning what we want, we make decisions. And in making those decisions, we take a certain amount of risk. For example, my husband is a civil engineer, and when he worked on major construction projects, we relocated to areas where the projects were. I spent the first twenty-seven years of my life in Pennsylvania. All of my family lived near Pittsburgh; most of my close friends were in the state. Our first relocation was to Dugway Proving Ground in Utah! Talk about a change, and talk about uncertainty. Would I be lonely moving to a place where I knew no one? Would I be able to get a job? Would I make friends? What would life be like as a civilian on a military base? What would life be like living in the desert? There was a lot at stake with the move, lots of risk for me.

Uncertainty is a factor in taking risks. So is the fear of failure. Failure is a lack of success, which is often construed as something negative. Mistakes are a form of failure. The chapter on savoring mistakes addressed how mistakes are learning opportunities, how they teach us; they are nothing more than an adjustment to the original plan. Failure must also be looked at in a positive light. Intentional risk taking means that we might fail, but we see a good chance for success or a positive outcome. (Intentional risk taking has been thought out and is being done for a purpose versus reckless risk taking that is done without thought or purpose.)

Intentional risk taking is done in a changed environment. Let's look at an example that combines uncertainty, concern about failure, and intentional risk taking. During the week my mother-in-law was scheduled to visit us in Oregon, I was scheduled to be at a College Reading and Learning Association (CRLA) board meeting in Sacramento, California. I decided to take my mother-in-law with me to the meeting. We would at least be able to visit with each other in the evenings. I love San Francisco, and it is only eighty-seven miles from Sacramento. I thought that would be a nice evening activity for my mother-in-law and me. So after a day of meetings, we, along with a colleague and her daughter, began our trek to San Francisco. We had a magnificent time.

At midnight, we decided to head back to Sacramento. It hadn't been long after leaving the parking garage when several dashboard lights came on. I searched for an open service station to seek help. The attendant was unable to provide any assistance, and he would not let me use a phone to call for help. He would not even make a call for me. This was before everyone carried cell phones, and as luck would have it, there was no pay phone nearby. What to do? What to do?

I noticed a tow truck driving up a nearby hill, so without thought, I started to chase it, yelling and waving my hands. I must have caught the driver's attention as he turned around and came back to me. The man who came out of the truck was big and burly (very scary to me). I explained my situation and pointed to where the car was. He said he would help.

Risk? Uncertainty? Indeed! Dark, nearly deserted section of San Francisco. Total stranger. Truly, a tow truck driver or someone disguised as one? Decisions. Decisions. However, I had a purpose. I needed to get three other people back to Sacramento. So I took the risk and decided to trust the tow truck driver. I walked and he followed to where the car was. He introduced himself as Mario. Mario checked under the hood and said the oil pan was missing. He would tow us to his garage.

I got behind the wheel of the car. Mario instructed me to not touch anything. He then looked at me and said, "Like hell you won't.

You come in the truck with me." What? Another risky decision to make. I decided nothing bad would happen with three other people around, so up into the cab of the tow truck I climbed (in my pristine white dress, nonetheless).

He towed us to one of Frisco's seedier sections of town, where sirens constantly serenaded and flashing police car lights provided background lighting. I was able to call the rental car company, who said they'd send another car for me. The four of us waited, not knowing what to expect.

The goal of getting my three companions safely back to Sacramento kept driving the decisions. The risks taken were all intentional. Every decision was made with the end result in mind: return safely to Sacramento. The story does have a positive conclusion. A replacement car was finally delivered around 4 a.m. We arrived in Sacramento at 6 a.m. At 8 a.m., my friend and I were back in a CRLA board meeting, somewhat sleep deprived but safe and sound.

We have all heard the proverb, "Nothing ventured, nothing gained." In times of change and transition, if we want to gain, to make progress in the new environment or situation, we must venture. With that venture, we will sometimes have to take risks to move forth, to make progress. If not a risk taker by nature, how does one develop this skill, this strategy?

1. Visualize the outcome. Know what is desired, what is wanted in the changed environment or situation. Focus on the outcome, and think about what steps or options will lead there.

2. Conduct an inquiry. Ask lots of questions. What is keeping me from achieving this outcome? What is keeping me from taking action to achieve this outcome? What do I fear? If I choose an action whose outcome is uncertain, how will I feel? What is the worst-case scenario? Are there roadblocks? What are they? Are there consequences to not pursuing the

outcome? What are the risks? Are there consequences of not taking the risk(s)? What happens if the action doesn't get me to the outcome? What are the pros and cons of the action?

3. Assess the risk. Always determine the appropriateness of the risk compared to the desired outcome. (The risk should be positive and should not put anyone in danger of being harmed.)

4. Consider alternatives. Are there different outcomes from the one identified? Are there consequences for doing nothing? List reasons for which the outcome doesn't deserve any risks being taken. What will life be like in the changed environment or situation if no risks are taken?

5. Take a walk on the wild side. Periodically, enjoy the unknown. Purposefully, step out of the comfort zone and experience something new. A friend's daughter recently got married and received a gift certificate for skydiving as a wedding present. She definitely stepped out of her comfort zone and took a walk on the wild side. While she hated every minute of the dive, she did learn that she could take a huge risk, that she could experience the unknown, that she could face her fears, and that she could learn from all of it.

6. Turn failures into learning opportunities. Just as my friend's daughter took her skydiving experience (not necessarily a failure but definitely something she didn't like) and turned it into a learning opportunity, so should we when a risk we've taken doesn't lead to or help the outcome. Determine what went wrong, and use that information to do something differently the next time around.

7. Practice relaxation techniques. If at any time in the decision-making process regarding taking a risk symptoms of stress appear, do something to relax. Meditate. Exercise. Practice deep-breathing exercises. Use visualization (of a favorite

or most relaxing place). Do progressive muscle-relaxation exercises. Engage in rhythmic exercise. Do yoga or tai chi. Go for a walk. Call a good friend/touchstone. Play with a pet. Get a massage. Take a long bath. Listen to music. Curl up with a good book. Light scented candles.

Reader Reflection

1. What does the strategy of taking risks involve?
2. Why would early explorers be considered risk takers?
3. What are some factors with risk taking?
4. What is the difference between intentional risk taking and reckless risk taking?
5. What is meant by "nothing ventured, nothing gained"?
6. Why is this strategy an important one when dealing with change/transition?
7. When would it be good to use this strategy?
8. Which of the development suggestions would be most effective for me? Why?
9. Am I facing a change where I might find myself needing to take risks?
10. Is this a skill I need to develop? If yes, select at least one of the suggestions from the above list to focus on.
11. How do I see myself using this strategy when dealing with change/transition?
12. Even if not undergoing a change or transition, how can I apply this strategy to my daily life to make it more meaningful, pleasant, and positive?

PRESERVING SANITY:
You Have to Dream Big

"Nothing happens unless first a dream."
—Carl Sandburg

IN THIS LAST STRATEGY for managing change and transition, dreams signify something one might fantasize about, something one is ambitious for, a desire, and an aspiration. For example, I have a dream of becoming a college president. Dreams are very similar to hopes. The difference is a subtle one. Hope is where one wants or expects something, especially something that is likely to happen. For example, I hope to be the candidate of choice for this presidential position.

Someone once said, "Hope is not a dream but a way of making dreams become reality." To turn dreams into reality, we must have hope along with action. Dreams will stay dreams unless the object of the dream is turned into action. I dream of becoming a college president, but unless I gain the experience needed for such a position, this aspiration will only remain a dream. One way to turn a dream into reality is by setting goals. Goals are our plans for the future. Goals are what we are trying to achieve. When we set goals, we determine what result we want and then we put forth effort to achieve that result.

Why are dreams important when managing change and transition? With change, something becomes different. We are moved out of the comfort zone. Our personal and professional lives can become unsettled. Dreams are a way of helping us deal with the unsettled nature of things. If we dream about something happening and really desire that to happen, we might work hard to make that dream come true. Dreams give us possibilities. Our dreams should be big! Small ones cannot ignite the flames of enthusiasm, excitement, and passion. Remember, anything that can be imagined can become reality under the right circumstances.

Take for example the story of Eileen Goudge (Cremona 1997). She was nineteen when her marriage failed and she had to raise a one-year-old son alone (the change for her). She received no child support and worked at a minimum-wage job that barely covered expenses. She had to apply for welfare to survive (the shift from her comfort zone). Eileen had no college degree and no professional skills. *But* she had a dream of being a writer. Eileen worked hard to turn her dream into a reality. In addition to writing when she could, she enrolled in a writing course. In an article, Neil Lewis, PhD, says, "Eileen Goudge succeeded as a writer because she looked inside herself and found her dream." He further states, "The most successful people set their dreams high then turn to their everyday life to find ways of achieving them." Today, Eileen is a millionaire writer. Her advice to others is this: "Keep dreaming because you *can* make those dreams come true" (Cremona 1997). We must live our dream just as Eileen is living hers.

At one point, Eileen thought her dream was far-fetched. That would have been true, had she not acted on her dream. In Eileen's case, dreams provided the impetus for her to take the action necessary to deal with the change and transition in her life. Just as Eileen did, dreams can be turned into achievable goals. Just talking about one's dream is step one in making it come true. And just as Eileen did, one must stop talking about the dream and take some action on it.

Becky Johnen

When this happens, the dream changes into a goal. Once the goal is established, steps to achieve it must be outlined. These steps become our "GPS unit," guiding us along the path that is moving that dream into a reality. (And just as a GPS unit will recalculate when a wrong turn is made, so too will we, at times, recalculate when the steps we've outlined need to be modified.)

You have to dream big. Whether someone is caught up in change or is an agent of change, dreaming big helps inspire others to do likewise. (For those undergoing change and transition, seeing others follow their dreams and being successful may be all the motivation that is needed to make a positive difference in their lives.) In her book *Things I Wish I'd Known Sooner: Personal Discoveries of a Mother of Twelve* (Edwards 1997), Jaroldeen Edwards relays a story of visiting her daughter. While taking her daughter to the garage to pick up a car, they took a detour along a mountain road. Edwards describes how they turned a corner and saw, from the top of the mountain, sloping for several acres across folds and valleys, rivers of daffodils in radiant bloom. She describes it as a profusion of color that blazed before them like a carpet. It looked as if the sun had tipped over and spilled gold down the mountainside. At the center of this scene, purple hyacinths were like a cascading waterfall. Coral-colored tulips were sprinkled throughout.

Edwards wondered who had created such beauty, why, and how. A sign at the center of the property indicated that "one woman, two hands, two feet, and very little brain, one at a time, started in 1958" had been responsible for that scene of beauty. Edwards relays that she was moved by what she had seen and by the realization that the woman who created the beautiful flower garden had changed the world one bulb at a time. Seeing this, Edwards talks of what things would have been like if she had a vision and worked at it just a little each day. What would she have accomplished?

The woman responsible for this creation of beauty probably started with a dream of what she hoped to accomplish. She acted on that dream and from 1958 through at least 1997 worked to accomplish her dream. In a way, the creator of the garden motivated Edwards and countless others who came upon the folds and valley of flowers.

Dreams help us navigate the waters of change and transition. On his 1991 album *Ropin' the Wind*, Garth Brooks has a ballad titled "The River." In this song, a river is used as a comparison to one's dreams. In the first stanza, Brooks writes,

> You know a dream is like a river, ever changin' as it flows. And the dreamer's just a vessel that must follow where it goes. Trying to learn from what's behind you, and never knowing what's in store makes each day a constant battle just to stay between the shores.

The chorus of the song tells us,

> And I will sail my vessel 'til the river runs dry. Like a bird upon the wind, these waters are my sky. I'll never reach my destination, if I never try. So I will sail my vessel 'til the river runs dry.

The second stanza continues,

> Too many times we stand aside and let the waters slip away, 'til what we put off 'til tomorrow has now become today. So don't you sit upon the shoreline and say you're satisfied. Choose to chance the rapids, and dare to dance the tide.

This song highlights the importance of pursuing our dreams. Brooks talks about never reaching one's destination if one doesn't even try. It is our dreams that provide the destination. Brooks talks about needing action to make the dreams a reality when he talks about not sitting upon the shoreline. And Brooks encourages us to take on any challenges along the way with his words "choose to chance the rapids and dare to dance the tide." Indeed, dreams are powerful and can set the stage for a new reality, especially in a changed environment or situation.

Tom Clancy sums everything up nicely when he says, "Nothing is as real as a dream. The world can change around you, but your dream will not. Responsibilities need not erase it. Duties need not obscure it. Because the dream is within you, no one can take it away" (Clancy 2013).

How do we go about developing this strategy, this skill of dreaming big?

1. Prepare a bucket list. If dreams for the future are elusive, start by preparing a bucket list. Many find this an easy exercise to do. The list is usually made up of things one wants to do before dying. This is a nice way of jump-starting the process of even thinking about dreams. As an example, I had on my bucket list meeting Steven Tyler of Aerosmith. In 2012, Aerosmith was on tour and the closest it came to Pittsburgh, Pennsylvania, was Cleveland, Ohio. Not knowing how much longer the band might be together and touring, I was determined to attend this concert. Not wanting to go alone, I took one of my childhood friends, treating her to an early "milestone" birthday present. Much planning and saving went into making this dream a reality. But it happened. On June 19, 2012, I not only got to meet Steven Tyler, but I convinced him to give me a birthday kiss—a dream fulfilled and an item off the bucket list!

2. Develop an interest inventory. Examples of items to include (not exhaustive by any means) are favorite things to do (by self and with friends), hobbies, special skills and abilities, proudest accomplishment, and dream job.

3. Explore something of interest. Sometimes, we do have a dream, but the confidence to pursue it is lacking. To determine whether the dream has merits, read more about it and observe someone doing something similar. Volunteer where that dream of yours may already be taking place.

4. Practice intentional daydreaming. Create a list of dreams. Prioritize the list.

5. Make the dream real. Select one of the dreams from the daydream list. Identify a goal related to that dream. Write down what it will take to reach that goal: who, what, where, when, why. Who needs to be involved? What needs to be done and when? What resources will be needed? What support is needed? Where will the dream be achieved? Why this dream? Why now?

6. Imagine the goal is accomplished. Ask, "How do I feel? Am I happy? Am I excited? What exactly am I doing? What does this accomplishment feel like? How are things in my life going to be different as a result of this accomplishment?" If you can see achievement of the dream/goal, it is more likely to actually happen.

7. Develop an appropriate mind-set. Whether creating the dream or working to make it a reality, one must be in the right frame of mind. This requires focus, persistence, and determination.

8. Practice positive self-talk. Sometimes, we are our own worst enemies when trying to accomplish something. Banish negative thoughts. Focus on being positive and optimistic.

9. Gain perspective. Talk to friends (especially touchstones) about the dream. Explain the dream. Doing this helps make it seem more real and worth pursuing. The more specific, the better.

Reader Reflection

1. Related to this strategy, what are dreams?
2. What is the difference between dreams and hopes?
3. How are dreams turned into reality?
4. Why are dreams important when managing change/transition?
5. Why should dreams be big?
6. In the song "The River," in what ways does Garth Brooks compare a river to dreams? How does this song highlight the importance of pursuing our dreams?
7. When would it be good to use this strategy?
8. Which of the development suggestions would be most effective for me? Why?
9. Am I facing a change where I might need to dream big?
10. Is this a skill I need to develop? If yes, select at least one of the suggestions from the above list to focus on.
11. How do I see myself using this strategy when dealing with change/transition?
12. Even if not undergoing a change or transition, how can I apply this strategy to my daily life to make it more meaningful, pleasant, and positive?

Conclusion

THE IDEAS AND CONCEPTS presented in this book are based on a presentation made at the College Reading and Learning Association's 1997 annual conference, whose theme was "Pearls of Wisdom." After watching staff and colleagues become frustrated, angry, depressed, fearful, and stressed over changes happening in postsecondary education, I knew I wanted the presentation to deal with change. The words of Helen Keller—"Keep your face to the sunshine and you will never see the shadow"—came to mind, and my presentation on change had its focus.

In Aerosmith's song "Tell Me" (from the *Music from Another Dimension!* CD), the phrase, "Oh I can tell the sun's still shinin' but the shadows are all I see" (Hamilton 2012) aptly describes what was happening to my staff and colleagues. While much good was happening (shining sun) as a result of the changes we were undergoing, those around me were only experiencing or seeing shadows, such as disbelief, frustration, anger, depression, fear, and stress. I wanted them to be able to deal more effectively and positively with the changes and the transitions. I wanted them to see beyond the shadows; I wanted them to experience the sunshine.

In order for my staff and colleagues to experience the sunshine, they first had to have ways of dealing with the shadows and what stood in their way. And to do that effectively, they had to take care of themselves first. They had to learn how to "put on their own oxygen mask" first.

The strategies presented in this book can serve as personal "oxygen masks." They can serve as ways to rejuvenate us when the challenges of change and transition become too much. How we respond to change and transition is more important than what happens to us in the changed environment. Oftentimes, the change is out of our control. We have little control over the events that shape our experience in the change and transition, but we do have choice over how we react and respond to the events in our life. However, we sometimes need help to develop more positive and appropriate responses to changes.

The concepts presented in this book are designed to provide such help. In *Facing the Sunshine and Avoiding the Shadows: Strategies to Stay Sane and Positive amid Change,* we have explored sixteen ways to face the sunshine and avoid the shadows; sixteen oxygen rejuvenators; sixteen ways to make a difference in our attitude, outlook, and motivational level; and sixteen ways to make a difference when dealing with current and future challenges. The acronym PRESERVING SANITY was used to present the strategies and to help with remembering them.

The following charts summarize the specific strategies and also provide a key phrase, word, image, or symbol to help with remembering the strategy. I hope this book provides just what is needed to preserve one's sanity in this ever-changing world.

Strategy	Key Point	Key Phrase, Word, Image, or Symbol
Persistence	The need to keep going even in the face of adversity	The force of the waves is in their persistence.
Relationships	The importance of always having someone who can serve as a "touchstone"; someone with whom one can discuss what is happening	Synergy created by two or more people
Enthusiasm	The need to remain positive and upbeat at all times	Young children at play
Sense of humor	The need to laugh a lot and often	The wedding dress scene and response
Ending something	All transitions or change begin with the ending of something	To get what you want, you must give up what is
Roaming the "wilderness"	The need to spend time in the "neutral zone," which is a gap between the old and the new	Watch for footprints in the snow: new ideas, discoveries, and creativity.
Vision	One's idea for what can be; new beginning	Seahorse seeking his fortune
Irreverent thinking	Divergent thinking; going beyond conventional wisdom	Lemming in an inner tube
Negotiating roadblocks	Ability to change course and direction when needed	*The Wizard of Oz* characters
Giggling	The need to laugh and laugh often	Hot, cold, good, and bad

Strategy	Key Point	Key Phrase, Word, Image, or Symbol
Savoring mistakes	Adopting the attitude that mistakes teach us; a mistake is nothing more than an adjustment to the plan	If you want to succeed, double your failure rate.
"Atta persons"	The need to frequently do random acts of kindness and let others know that they are appreciated	Blue ribbons
New style of thinking	Kaleidoscopic thinking— forming new patters from existing data and resources	Kaleidoscope
Innovativeness	Thinking creatively and outside the box	Don't let habits get in the way of new thoughts.
Taking risks	Only those who will risk going too far can possibly find out how far one can go.	Early explorers
You have to dream big!	The need to set goals, not limit them, and pursue the goals in earnest	Eileen Goudge, Jaroldeen Edwards, and the flower-filled mountaintop

Reader Reflection

IMMEDIATELY AFTER READING THIS book, respond to the following statements.

1. The next time I am faced with a change in my life (whether it is seismic, major, or minor), one of the first things I will do is _____.
2. In the next month, I will display my "gratitude attitude" by _____.
3. The next time I am faced with a "roadblock," I will _____.
4. A dream I have is _____.
5. I will work on making my dream by _____.
6. My perfect day is _____.

One month after reading this book, reflect on the following questions.

1. What changes have I faced in the last month?

2. Have I used any of the strategies?
3. Which ones have worked the best for me?
4. Which ones have brought a smile to my heart?
5. Have I had occasion to need a touchstone, and if so, have I reached out to someone?
6. Even if I have not undergone a change or transition, did I apply any of the strategies to my daily life to make it more meaningful, pleasant, and positive?

About the Author

BECKY JOHNEN, EDD, IS a recently retired educational administrator who now provides consulting services on strategic planning, leadership, standards, teaching and learning, program assessment, curriculum, and dealing with change to community organizations, civic groups, businesses, nonprofit organizations, and educational organizations.

She is the developer of *Challenging Adults to Read Effectively: A Guide for Teachers and Tutors*, a contributing author to the EDL workbook series Reading Strategies and Thinking Strategies, and has published journal articles on learning difficulties and disabilities, strategic planning, and the politics of leadership. She is a frequent presenter at education-related conferences.

She earned a bachelor's degree in the education of exceptional children from The Pennsylvania State University, a master's of education degree and a reading specialist certificate from Elmira College, and a doctorate in adult education from Nova Southeastern University. She has been a middle school and high school classroom teacher and an instructor at community colleges and universities, and she has served in a variety of community college administrative positions. She has also served as head of school at a private K–12 academy.

Becky currently resides in southwest Pennsylvania with her husband, Bob, and nephew, John Michael. In addition to her consulting work, she delivers monthly informational, inspirational, and motivational presentations as part of her church's Bethany Ministry program.

References

Benson, Herbert, MD. *The Relaxation Response.* New York: Morrow, 1975.

Berkun, Scott. "How to Learn from Your Mistakes." Accessed June 23, 2013. http://scottberkun.com/essays/44-how-to-learn-from-your-mistakes/.

Bianchi, Sue, Jan Butler, David Richey, and Sue Bianchi. *Warmups for Meeting Leaders.* San Diego: University Associates, 1990.

Bridges, William. *Managing Transitions: Making the Most of Change.* Reading, MA: Addison-Wesley, 1991.

_____. *Transitions: Making Sense of Life's Changes.* Cambridge, MA: Da Capo Press, 2004.

Brooks, Garth. "The River." In *Ropin' the Wind.* 1991, Vinyl recording.

Carlson, Richard. *Don't Sweat the Small Stuff ... and It's All Small Stuff: Simple Ways to Keep the Little Things from Taking Over Your Life.* New York: Hyperion, 1997.

Clancy, Tom. "Tom Clancy Quotations." Thinkexist. Accessed June 30, 2013. http://en.thinkexist.com/quotes/Tom_Clancy/.

Cremona, Sherry. "Storybook Ending." *Woman's World*, January 14, 1997, 6.

Edison, Thomas A. "Thomas A. Edison Quotations." Thinkexist. Accessed June 23, 2013. http://en.thinkexist.com/quotes/thomas_alva_edison/.

Edwards, Jaroldeen. *Things I Wish I'd Known Sooner: Personal Discoveries of a Mother of Twelve*. New York: Pocket Books, 1997.

Einstein, Albert. "Albert Einstein Quotations." Thinkexist. Accessed June 25, 2013. http://thinkexist.com/quotes/Albert_Einstein/.

Eliot, T. S. "T. S. Eliot Quotations." Thinkexist. Accessed July 2, 2013. http://thinkexist.com/quotes/t.s._eliot/.

Emmons, Robert A. *Gratitude Works! A 21-Day Program for Creating Emotional Prosperity*. San Francisco: Jossey-Bass, 2013.

Freud, Sigmund. "Humor." *International Journal of Psychoanalysis* 9 (1928): 1–6.

Guilford, J. P. *The Nature of Human Intelligence*. New York: McGraw-Hill, 1967.

Hamilton, Tom. "Tell Me." In *Music from Another Dimension!* Aerosmith. Columbia Records, 2012, CD.

Holmes, Oliver W. "Oliver Wendell Holmes, Jr. Quotations." Thinkexist. Accessed June 22, 2013. http://thinkexist.com/quotes/oliver_wendell_holmes,_jr./.

Jordan, Michael. "Michael Jordan Quotations." Thinkexist. Accessed June 23, 2013. http://thinkexist.com/quotations/obstacles/2.html.

Kanter, Rosabeth M. "Rosabeth Moss Kanter Quotations." Thinkexist. Accessed June 23, 2013. http://en.thinkexist.com/quotes/ rosabeth_moss_kanter/.

Keller, Helen. "Helen Keller Quotations." Helen Keller Quotes. Accessed June 30, 2013. http://en.thinkexist.com/quotes/ helen_keller/2.html.

Kübler-Ross, Elisabeth, and David Kessler. *On Grief and Grieving: Finding the Meaning of Grief through the Five Stages of Loss.* New York: Scribner, 2005.

Landers, Ann. "Ann Landers Quotations." Thinkexist. Accessed July 2, 2013. http://en.thinkexist.com/quotes/ann_landers/.

Legace, Martha. "From Tigers to Kaleidoscopes: Thinking about Future Leadership." *Working Knowledge,* May 21, 2001. Accessed June 29, 2013. http://hbswk.hbs.edu/item/2245. html.

Luks, Allan. "The Healing Power of Doing Good: The Health and Spiritual Benefits of Helping Others." Barnes & Noble. 2001. Accessed June 24, 2013. http://www.barnesandnoble.com/w/ the-healing-power-of-doing-good-allan-luks/1112722414.

Mayo Clinic, Staff. "Stress Basics." Mayo Clinic. March 19, 2011. Accessed June 24, 2013. http://www.mayoclinic.com/ health/stress-management/MY00435.

Pavlina, Steve. "Self-Discipline: Persistence." Self-Discipline: Persistence. Accessed June 20, 2013. http://www. stevepavlina.com/blog/2006/self-discipline-persistence/.

Peale, Norman V. "Norman Vincent Peale Quotations." Thinkexist. Accessed July 1, 2013. http://en.thinkexist.com/quotes/ norman_vincent_peale/.

Robbins, Anthony. "Anthony Robbins Quotations." Thinkexist. Accessed June 25, 2013. http://thinkexist.com/quotes/anthony_robbins/.

Salmansohn, Karen. "The Up Side: Quotes from Today's Positive Thinkers." *Guideposts*, July 2013, 24.

Sandburg, Carl. "Carl Sandburg Quotations." Thinkexist. Accessed July 2, 2013. http://en.thinkexist.com/search/searchquotation.asp?search=carl+sandburg+quotations.

Sheehy, Gail. "Gail Sheehy Quotations." Thinkexist. Web. Accessed July 2, 2013. http://en.thinkexist.com/quotes/gail_sheehy/.

Sinetar, Marsha. "Marsha Sinetar Quotations." Thinkexist. Accessed June 23, 2013. http://thinkexist.com/quotations/obstacles/.

Watson, Thomas. "Thomas Watson Quotations." My Inspirational Quotes. Accessed July 2, 2013. http://www.my-inspirational-quotes.com/quotes-on-failures/double-failure/.

Bibliography

Benson, Herbert, MD. *The Relaxation Response*. New York: Morrow, 1975.

Berkun, Scott. "How to Learn from Your Mistakes." Accessed June 23, 2013. http://scottberkun.com/essays/44-how-to-learn-from-your-mistakes/.

Bianchi, Sue, Jan Butler, David Richey, and Sue Bianchi. *Warmups for Meeting Leaders*. San Diego: University Associates, 1990.

Bridges, William. *Managing Transitions: Making the Most of Change*. Reading, MA: Addison-Wesley, 1991.

_____. *Transitions: Making Sense of Life's Changes*. Cambridge, MA: Da Capo Press, 2004.

Brooks, Garth. "The River." In *Ropin' the Wind*. 1991, Vinyl recording.

Carlson, Richard. *Don't Sweat the Small Stuff ... and It's All Small Stuff: Simple Ways to Keep the Little Things from Taking Over Your Life*. New York: Hyperion, 1997.

Clancy, Tom. "Tom Clancy Quotations." Thinkexist. Accessed June 30, 2013. http://en.thinkexist.com/quotes/Tom_Clancy/.

Cremona, Sherry. "Storybook Ending." *Woman's World,* January 14, 1997, 6.

Edison, Thomas A. "Thomas A. Edison Quotations." Thinkexist. Accessed June 23, 2013. http://en.thinkexist.com/quotes/ thomas_alva_edison/.

Edwards, Jaroldeen. *Things I Wish I'd Known Sooner: Personal Discoveries of a Mother of Twelve.* New York: Pocket Books, 1997.

Einstein, Albert. "Albert Einstein Quotations." Thinkexist. Accessed June 25, 2013. http://thinkexist.com/quotes/Albert_ Einstein/.

Eliot, T. S. "T. S. Eliot Quotations." Thinkexist. Accessed July 2, 2013. http://thinkexist.com/quotes/t.s._eliot/.

Emmons, Robert A. *Gratitude Works! A 21-Day Program for Creating Emotional Prosperity.* San Francisco: Jossey-Bass, 2013.

_____. *Thanks! How the New Science of Gratitude Can Make You Happier.* Boston: Houghton Mifflin, 2007.

"Friendship Facts, Information, Pictures/Encyclopedia.com articles about Friendship." Encyclopedia.com. Accessed June 12, 2013. http://www.encyclopedia.com/topic/Friendship.aspx.

Freud, Sigmund. "Humor." *International Journal of Psychoanalysis* 9 (1928): 1–6.

Gallozzi, Chuck. "Dreams and Goals." Dreams and Goals. May 1, 2010. Accessed June 30, 2013. http://www.personal-development.com/chuck/dreams-goals.htm.

Guilford, J. P. *The Nature of Human Intelligence.* New York: McGraw-Hill, 1967.

Hamilton, Tom. "Tell Me." In *Music from Another Dimension!* Aerosmith. Columbia Records, 2012, CD.

Heathfield, Susan. "Achieve Your Dreams: 6 Steps to Accomplish Your Goals and Resolutions." About.com Human Resources. Accessed June 30, 2013. http://humanresources.about.com/od/strategicplanning1/a/goal_setting.htm.

Holmes, Oliver W. "Oliver Wendell Holmes, Jr. Quotations." Thinkexist. Accessed June 22, 2013. http://thinkexist.com/quotes/oliver_wendell_holmes,_jr./.

"How to Maintain a Sense of Humor to Cope with Stress." Stress and Stress Management—Causes, Symptoms, Stress Relief Tips, and Stress Tests. Accessed June 12, 2103. http://stress.about.com/od/positiveattitude/ht/humor.htm.

Jordan, Michael. "Michael Jordan Quotations." Thinkexist. Accessed June 23, 2013. http://thinkexist.com/quotations/obstacles/2.html.

Kanter, Rosabeth M. *The Change Masters: Innovation and Entrepreneurship in the American Corporation.* New York: Simon & Schuster, 1984.

_____. "Kaleidoscopic Thinking." In *Management 21C, Someday We'll All Manage This Way,* edited by S. Chowdhury, 250–261.

Saddle River, NJ: Prentice Hall Financial Times , 2000.

_____. "Rosabeth Moss Kanter Quotations." Thinkexist. Accessed June 23, 2013. http://en.thinkexist.com/quotes/rosabeth_moss_kanter/.

Keller, Helen. "Helen Keller Quotations." Helen Keller Quotes. Accessed June 30, 2013. http://en.thinkexist.com/quotes/helen_keller/2.html.

Kübler-Ross, Elisabeth, and David Kessler. *On Grief and Grieving: Finding the Meaning of Grief through the Five Stages of Loss.* New York: Scribner, 2005.

Landers, Ann. "Ann Landers Quotations." Thinkexist. Accessed July 2, 2013. http://en.thinkexist.com/quotes/ann_landers/.

Legace, Martha. "From Tigers to Kaleidoscopes: Thinking about Future Leadership." *Working Knowledge,* May 21, 2001. Accessed June 29, 2013. http://hbswk.hbs.edu/item/2245.html.

Luks, Allan. "The Healing Power of Doing Good: The Health and Spiritual Benefits of Helping Others." Barnes & Noble. 2001. Accessed June 24, 2013. http://www.barnesandnoble.com/w/the-healing-power-of-doing-good-allan-luks/1112722414.

Lyubomirsky, Sonja. *The How of Happiness: A Scientific Approach to Getting the Life You Want.* New York: Penguin Press, 2008.

Mayo Clinic, Staff. "Stress Basics." Mayo Clinic. March 19, 2011. Accessed June 12, 2013. http://www.mayoclinic.com/health/stress-management/MY00435.

Pavlina, Steve. "Self-Discipline: Persistence." Self-Discipline: Persistence. Accessed June 20, 2013. http://www.stevepavlina.com/blog/2006/self-discipline-persistence/.

Peale, Norman V. "Norman Vincent Peale Quotations." Thinkexist. Accessed July 1, 2013. http://en.thinkexist.com/quotes/norman_vincent_peale/.

Rath, Tom. *Vital Friends: The People You Can't Afford to Live Without.* New York: Gallup Press, 2006.

Robbins, Anthony. "Anthony Robbins Quotations." Thinkexist. Accessed June 25, 2013. http://thinkexist.com/quotes/anthony_robbins/.

Rye, Suzann. "Why Mistakes Are Good for Us." Self-Growth.com. 2009. Accessed June 23, 2013. http://www.selfgrowth.com/articles/Why_Mistakes_Are_Good_for_Us.html.

Salmansohn, Karen. "The Up Side: Quotes from Today's Positive Thinkers." *Guideposts*, July 2013, 24.

Sandburg, Carl. "Carl Sandburg Quotations." Thinkexist. Accessed July 2, 2013. http://en.thinkexist.com/search/searchquotation.asp?search=carl+sandburg+quotations.

Seligman, Martin E. P. *Authentic Happiness: Using the New Positive Psychology to Realize Your Potential for Lasting Fulfillment.* New York: Free Press, 2002.

Sheehy, Gail. "Gail Sheehy Quotations." Thinkexist. Accessed July 2, 2013. http://en.thinkexist.com/quotes/gail_sheehy/.

Sinetar, Marsha. "Marsha Sinetar Quotations." Thinkexist. Accessed June 23, 2013. http://thinkexist.com/quotations/obstacles/.

Smith, Melinda, MA, and Jeanne Segal, PhD. "Laughter Is the Best Medicine." HelpGuide.org. May 2013. Accessed June 12, 2013. http://www.helpguide.org/life/humor_laughter_health.htm.

Smith, Melinda, MA, Robert Segal, MA, and Jeanne Segal, PhD. "Stress Symptoms, Signs, and Causes: The Effects of Stress Overload and What You Can Do about It." HelpGuide.org.

May 2013. Accessed June 12, 2013. http://helpguide.org/mental/stress_signs.htm.

Vernon, Mark. *The Philosophy of Friendship*. Basingstoke: Palgrave Macmillan, 2005.

Watson, Thomas. "Thomas Watson Quotations." My Inspirational Quotes. Accessed July 2, 2013. http://www.my-inspirational-quotes.com/quotes-on-failures/double-failure/.

Wright, Paul H. "Toward a Theory of Friendship Based on a Conception of Self." *Human Communication Research* 4, no. 3 (1978): 196–207.

CPSIA information can be obtained at www.ICGtesting.com
Printed in the USA
BVOW01s0139300414

352035BV00001B/4/P

9 781462 407460